IN THE IRONS

IN THE IRONS

SHOW JUMPING, DRESSAGE AND EVENTING IN NORTH AMERICA

GARY J. BENSON
WITH PHIL MAGGITTI

CONCEPT BY SUSAN STILGENBAUER BENSON

HOWELL BOOK HOUSE • NEW YORK

Also by Gary J. Benson:
Rolling Thunder: A Portrait of North American Railroading
The Art of Railroad Photography

Howell Book House
A Prentice Hall Macmillan Company
15 Columbus Circle
New York, NY 10023

Library of Congress Cataloging-in-Publication Data
Benson, Gary J.
        In the irons : show jumping, dressage, and eventing
    in North America / Gary J. Benson with Phil Maggitti ;
    concept by Susan Stilgenbauer Benson.
            p.   cm.
        ISBN 0-87605-967-1
        1. Show jumping—United States.   2. Dressage—
    United States.   3. Eventing (Horsemanship)—United
    States.   I. Maggiti, Phil.   II. Title
    SF295.55.U6B45   1994   94-12282
                                              CIP

Book design: Jennifer Dossin

Book layout: Susan Hood

10   9   8   7   6   5   4   3   2   1

Manufactured in the United States of America

Facing Contents:
*Diana Miller and Calvin execute an extended trot across
the diagonal during their FEI Intermediate test at the 1994
Winter Equestrian Festival in Wellington, Florida.*

This book is dedicated to all who share the love of horses, the passion to ride and the drive to compete.

In the Irons was made possible, in part, by generous support from

We also wish to thank

Gladstone, NJ   New Canaan, CT

for their contribution to this project.

CONTENTS

FOREWORD

All riders are motivated by a love of horses and a desire to win, but the skills required in dressage, show jumping and three-day eventing are enormously different. Dressage riders need to pay keen attention to the intricate details of their tests. Three-day eventers have to be tremendously brave to ride miles over cross-country courses, jumping natural obstacles that do not yield when horses hit them. Jumper riders must develop extremely specialized technical skills to negotiate complex courses with precise distances between jumps. But no matter what the discipline, riding is ultimately an intellectual as well as an athletic endeavor.

The horse provides the athletic effort. The rider is the brains of the operation, the on-board computer making swift and often subtle adjustments as the competition progresses. There has always been a strong bond between man and horse. In equine sports that bond is more highly refined than in any other venture.

Riders have to know their horses emotionally and physically, and from that knowledge develop a strategy peculiar to each horse because each horse performs best from its own unique combination of stride length, impulsion and center of balance.

Furthermore, horses have distinct personalities. One horse might have to work on the longe line before starting flat work in preparation for a class. Another horse that's lacking in energy might go right from the stall to the ring in order to keep his enthusiasm high and his nerves sharp.

Riders also have to prepare themselves for competition by analyzing the course and performing the required test mentally, step by step, many times beforehand. A grand prix rider must have a plan as to how he wants to meet each jump in terms of speed, distance and angle, as well as a plan for the pace and balance needed between each jump. Riders have to visualize themselves performing every move flawlessly in order to develop a mental expectation of the ride.

Left
Leslie Lenehan and Fortus at the 1990 American Gold Cup in Devon, Pennsylvania. Lenehan rode on the United States Equestrian Team's gold medal-winning show-jumping contingents at the 1983 Pan-American Games in Caracas and the 1984 Olympic Games in Los Angeles. She also has won many individual honors, including the American Grandprix Association's 1983 Rider of the Year award, the 1986 World Cup Finals and the American Horse Shows Association's 1986 Horsewoman of the Year award. Many of her trips to the winner's circle have been made on a talented jumper named Pressurized and, more recently, on Gem Twist.

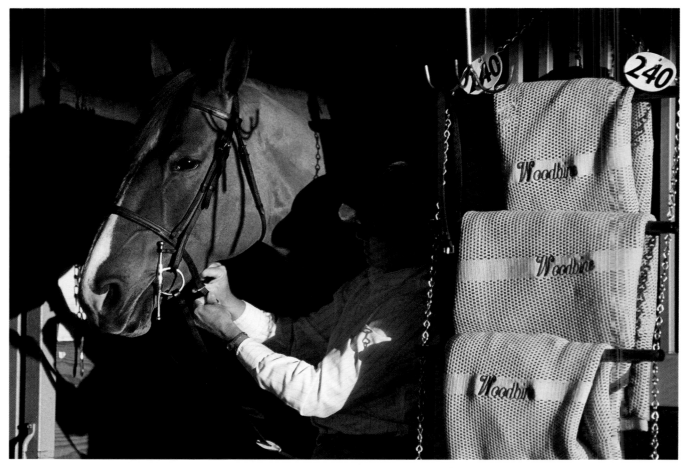

Sari Clapperton from Woodbine Farm in Michigan adjusts the noseband on her horse's bridle before competing in an early-morning class at the Winter Equestrian Festival in West Palm Beach, Florida.

No matter how different their individual skills, all riders are alike in their abiding love of horses. Like your first love, your first horse is an experience you never forget. Mine was a Shetland Pony named Topper that my parents leased for me when I was four. We brought him home, tied him in our yard, and there he lived for the summer. It was one of the happiest summers of my life.

A year or so later I competed in an under saddle class at my first show. There were half a dozen kids in the class, and I was the only one who didn't get a ribbon. After the other riders had been pinned and sent around the ring, the show officials had to ask me to leave.

When I started getting ribbons, I wasn't terribly struck by whether they were blue, red or yellow. I just wanted to ride. I think it is that quality—wanting to ride more than anything else—that separates horse people from all the rest.

As I learned to ride, I learned that there is no room for nerves in the show ring. The more emotions you have, the more errors you're going to commit. Horses are schooled to react to the rider, so a nervous rider sending erratic and inconsistent signals to his horse will only hinder his chances of a successful performance in the ring. I tell my students when they start to ride badly due to pressure, "This is a hard enough sport, don't go beating yourself."

When I enter the ring, I tune out everything else. I know that the ring announcer introduces each rider with a brief biographical description, but I haven't heard one yet. Of course, it's hard not to be aware of the crowd cheering you during a jumpoff. But to react to the crowd would be the worst thing of all. Reactions based on nerves rather than on strategy will only inhibit your performance.

I'm the same way around the barn. People kid me about going into my teaching trance, blocking out everything around me—conversations, distractions, the nervous parent blathering in my ear.

Participation in horse shows has grown tremendously during the eighteen years I've been riding professionally, but there is still room for additional growth. People who are considering taking part in dressage, three-day eventing or show jumping should not stay on the sidelines because they do not think they have the talent to compete in these sports. Talent is important, but there's no substitute for hard work. To succeed in this business—at any level—you have to be determined to work harder than the next person. Even though I won the Maclay when I was fifteen, I never thought of myself as overly talented. There were other riders who, I felt, had more talent; but I knew that if I worked hard enough, I could make up for that.

In addition to hard work and talent, the ability to get along with people is the third key ingredient for success in the horse world. There is great camaraderie within the horse community. Seldom do you find riders engaging in the "trash talking" popular in some other sports. All of us realize that hard work and dedication are the only keys to success, and for this reason riders have a mutual appreciation and respect for the success of their peers.

In that regard, I consider *In the Irons* a personal scrapbook for horse lovers: a beautiful and skilled production that is, above all, a warm, intimate portrait of the horse world, from schooling ring to show ring. Gary Benson's cameras are the readers' eyes, allowing horse lovers everywhere to experience the drama of the show world in a way that few people ever get to do.

LESLIE BURR LENEHAN

INTRODUCTION

When Americans handed the reins of government to a horse-riding president in 1980, by a happy coincidence most equine sports in this country took off at a gallop. Membership in the American Horse Shows Association (AHSA), which stood at roughly 34,000 on Inauguration Day 1981, grew to 55,000 by decade's end. During the same period, the number of shows licensed by AHSA registered a 45-percent increase, to a total of 2,500 shows a year. Other measures of performance—including number of competitors, attendance at shows and sponsors' participation—also demonstrate that horse sports enjoyed a popular landslide in the 1980s. And nowhere was that enjoyment more tangible than in show jumping, dressage and three-day eventing, which are the focus of this book.

The origins of the current popularity of these Olympic disciplines are rooted in the aftermath of World War II. Indeed, the modern history of show jumping, dressage and three-day eventing begins with the transfer of command from military to civilian riders following the war. By then, the four-legged horsepower that had supported the United States military had been replaced by the four-wheeled kind. Because horses were no longer important to the nation's defense, the cavalry school that had trained the military's horsemen and had produced, as a quadrennial byproduct, our Olympic equestrian teams since 1912 was disbanded.

To fill the empty saddles and to preserve the legacy that had been preserved by generations of military riders, the United States Equestrian Team (USET) was organized in 1950. Not surprisingly, former cavalrymen served as the first coaches and advisers for the USET, easing the transition in much the same way that an outgoing administration cooperates with its successor.

The military influence is apparent no longer in the modern show ring or on a cross-country course, but it is echoed in many equestrian traditions. The annual presentation of the Wofford Cup, for example, honors the memory of Colonel John W. Wofford, the USET's inaugural president. This award is given to the nonriding member of the United States Combined Training

Left
The last American to win a world championship—and the only rider to win back-to-back world titles—Bruce Davidson and his red-and-yellow Chesterland Farm colors are high flyers in the eventing world. At the 1990 Radnor Hunt International Three-Day Event, Davidson and Happy Talk exit the water over Carl's Climb on the advanced cross-country course.

Association (USCTA) who has done the most to further the progress of eventing.

Because the USET had been established to recruit and to train riders for international competition in dressage, show jumping and three-day eventing, other organizations dedicated to the stateside pursuit of happiness in these sports were created. The first was the United States Pony Clubs, Inc., founded in 1954. Fashioned after British and Canadian models, the Pony Club was critical to the development of eventing and of all-around horsemanship in this country, serving as a training ground where future competitors learned basic riding and stable-management skills. In that regard, membership in the Pony Club took the place of military service in many a young rider's life.

The fortunes of eventing have been guided formally by the USCTA, which was organized at a meeting held during the 1959 Pan-American Games in Chicago. The USCTA was created at the end of a transitional decade in eventing, just ten years after the first civilian had been allowed to compete in a three-day event in this country. For their part, the three decades that followed the establishment of the USCTA were a time of promise and development (the 1960s), of glittering success (the 1970s) and of impressive growth (the 1980s).

While the USET's three-day squad was winning gold medals at the 1974 World Championships and the 1976 Olympics, participation in three-day events was flourishing. Between 1972 and 1976, the number of two-day horse trials and full-scale events in the United States nearly tripled, and by 1976 there were more than three times as many active event riders than there had been four years before. That growth was amplified during the 1980s, and at the end of the decade nearly 25,000 entries were recorded in 225 USCTA-sanctioned events.

Meanwhile, similar growth occurred in dressage. Although it is fundamental to the development of any horse—no matter what its breeding, disposition or ultimate use—dressage is more of a singular pursuit than a spectator sport, more like solitaire than table-stakes poker. In dressage, riders compete against a standard of perfection, not directly against each other, and there is little of the drama to be found in the speed-and-endurance phase of a three-day event or the jumpoff in a grand prix competition.

Nevertheless, the United States Dressage Federation (USDF), founded in 1973, lays claim to being the largest organization to represent a single Olympic equestrian discipline. Individual membership in USDF, which more than doubled during the 1980s, stands at nearly 23,000. The number of AHSA/USDF-approved competitions, which increased by 158 percent during the last decade, is approaching 600.

This figure does not include local, nonsanctioned competitions, nor do any figures properly explain the appeal of the most subtle of equestrian activities. That attraction was articulated well by the rider who said, "At first I thought dressage was just warmup for cross-country, but then I learned to love the detail of dressage. There's nothing like it."

Without intending any slight to other equestrian sports, one might say that the flying Pegasus of the equine world during the 1980s was show jumping. Red hot and red coated, show jumping's ne plus ultra, grand prix competition, has angled its way onto the nation's television screens and into its sports pages, where jumping's high-dollar profile and million-dollar performers have caught the public's attention.

The reasons for show jumping's rise are several: It is an attractive sport to watch; it fits neatly into a stadium setting; it is amendable to television coverage—being about the same length as a football game; and it is easy for even novice spectators to keep score.

Like dressage and combined training, show jumping was schooled in the military academy, but unlike its Olympic counterparts, jumping has obtained an MBA—for major box-office attraction. In 1980, the two-year-old American Grandprix Association (AGA) sponsored eighteen events. Ten years later it sponsored thirty-one. In the interim, total AGA attendance had more than quadrupled, total prize money offered had nearly quintupled, the television audience had septupled and sponsorship income had increased tenfold—a quantum leap. Such was the appeal of grand prix jumping that besides the AGA's thirty-plus-event schedule each year, almost thirty other grand prixs are now sponsored annually by the National Grand Prix League (NGL), founded in 1989.

Although mechanization had rendered the horse

Lendon Gray of Bedford, New York, and Later On perform a piaffe across center line between passage movements during the Grand Prix test at the 1990 Miller's/United States Equestrian Team's National Dressage Championship held in Gladstone, New Jersey. Gray has won more national championships, nearly thirty, than any other U.S. rider. She was also a member of the USET's Olympic dressage team for the alternate Olympics in 1980 and the Seoul Olympics in 1988. One of Gray's most memorable horses was the unique Seldom Seen, a 14.3-hand Thoroughbred-Connemara cross who competed successfully at the Grand Prix level for five years.

obsolete as the soldier's working partner by the end of World War I, postwar prosperity afforded the leisure time for civilian riders to develop a sporting partnership with the horse. That alliance has been nurtured at countless barns and riding schools by persons of varying estates and occupations, persons for whom horses are a way of life, not a way of making a living. In truth, it is the workaday rider on whom the horse industry depends: the schoolteacher who competes in amateur owner classes, the parents who start the kids in leadline or short stirrup, the teenager who mucks out stalls in exchange for lessons, the executive who attends clinics taught by professional riders, the accountant who volunteers to sell programs at the local club's show and the devotees who read the horse magazines. These enthusiasts fill the stands at Devon and Palm Beach, Spruce Meadows and Indio, the National and Gladstone, Lexington and Upperville, and thou-

Two-time American Grandprix Association Rider of the Year Margie Goldstein and Daydream on their way toward winning the $50,000 Grandprix of Pittsburgh at the 1992 Hartwood Show Jumping Festival. Goldstein joined the grand prix circuit in 1985, bringing with her a love for jokes and hard work. In the spring of 1990 a horse fell on her, crushing all the bones in her left foot. Doctors said she would never walk normally again and would not be riding anytime soon, but Goldstein was back in the saddle a week later and back in competition nine weeks after that, riding with one stirrup and an ankle brace at first. The following year she won a record eight grand prixs.

sands of places each year from the backyard where proud parents wield camcorders to the A circuit grand prixs where sports networks deploy their film crews.

The allegiance of the workaday rider and equestrian fan has attracted, too, the increased participation of sponsors at major events. Sponsors beneficence to the American Grandprix Association increased by $1.2 million between 1980 and 1990. That increase accounted for 86 percent of the growth in purses and year-end awards offered by AGA during that same period. In all, $4 million in sponsors' largess gilds the coffers of dressage, three-day events and grand prix competitions each year.

Purveyors of fine wines and spirits, luxury automobiles, select watches and jewelry, and modish apparel were among the early sponsors of equestrian events. In time, banks, insurance companies, food provisioners, a few horse magazines and other entrepreneurs with an eye on what marketing experts call the upscale audience joined the congregation. Some sponsors even have begun subsidizing individual horses, a long-standing custom in Europe.

The growth among horse sports was such in the post–World War II years that each decade seemed to constitute its own generation. Without question the horse world in the 1980s reflected the go-go spirit of the economic and political worlds, and as the 1990s struggle to discover and assert their own character, those parallels appear to be continuing.

"Since 1990, equestrian sports have been going through the same shaking-out process that's happening all across the country," says one well-traveled course designer. "During the opulent eighties there was no shortage of people eager to spend money in the horse business. Now people are better informed and more particular. They're more discerning about where they choose to go and more demanding about the quality they expect to see and the special touches that make one show different from the others."

Consolidation and refinement follow any period of growth—and form the basis for continued expansion in the future. During this decade the equestrian community must find ways to retain the new exhibitors and fans it has attracted, in addition to finding ways to attract additional participants to equine sports. Horse show organizers have created new divisions and types of classes—the NGL's Adult Amateur Jumper Series is one example—designed to give more riders access to the kind of competition that fits their budgets, abilities and schedules. Additional schooling classes for jumpers, new classes for adult and children's hunters and jumpers, team competitions for adult novice combined-training competitors and "green as grass" dressage classes will allow more people than ever to experience the exhilaration of competing in a horse show. By welcoming newcomers while preserving established traditions, horse sports in the post–Cold War decades can solidify the remarkable gains made during the last forty years.

Riding before an enthusiastic audience, Penny Zavitz and Winsome demonstrate their winning technique in the 1994 FEI Grand Prix Freestyle competition held at West Palm Beach, Florida. Zavitz, a Toronto resident, won the Young Rider Gold Medal in 1984 and the Canadian Young Rider Championships in 1986. With Winsome, a 17.2-hand Hanoverian, she went on to win the North American Grand Prix Championships in 1993 and continued to compete successfully in 1994, representing Canada at the World Cup in Sweden.

IN THE IRONS

SHOW JUMPING

While the last remnants of night, congealed into droplets of water, cling to the wet grass, the first arrivals plod drowsily into the show grounds like early worshipers at church. Doors close, tailgates clank and tack boxes are hauled to their destinations. Horses are sleepwalked into wakefulness, boots are pulled on and hunt caps are donned with conviction. Scenes from a horse show morning. Your Town, USA.

A fourteen-year-old biting her lip while waiting to ride in a Medal class at Devon, Pennsylvania; a third grader in the green pony division in Bloomfield Hills, Michigan; a thirty-six-year-old grand prix rider walking the course before the American Invitational in Tampa, Florida; a "twenty-something" housewife riding in the adult jumper division in San Diego, California: faces at a horse show, faces enlivened by a love of horses and inspired by a love of competition.

From the smallest tot in a leadline class to the United States Equestrian Team member accepting a medal at the Olympics, everyone who takes part in horse shows takes part in The Life, a life that has its own statutes and vocabulary, its own rewards and icons, its own celebrities and raison d'être, a grand and elegant enterprise carried along on an irresistible undertow.

One ex-junior rider who gave up The Life for college and a regular job—only to sign on with a teaching barn before she turned thirty—describes the enchantment of The Life. "When you're out there doing flatwork all afternoon in the schooling ring, you know exactly what you're supposed to be doing. There isn't anything else in the world that matters. It's probably the only time in your life when you're in such complete control."

Greg Best, who rode the otherworldly Gem Twist to three Grandprix Association Horse of the Year titles and to double silver medals in the 1988 Olympics, elaborates on that theme. "The feeling that comes from being on a horse is analogous to the feeling you get from the horse world as a whole. If you're a horse person, you travel in circles and lead an existence that

Left
Anne Kursinski, a Californian who now lives in Flemington, New Jersey, and Cannonball at the first selection trial for the 1992 Olympic team, held at United States Equestrian Team headquarters in Gladstone, New Jersey. Kursinski was a member of the 1992 and 1988 Olympic teams and was an alternate member of the 1984 team. An instructor at George Morris's Hunterdon, Incorporated, Kursinski and the stallion Starman have been consistent winners on the grand prix circuit.

is very much isolated. This is a world where everybody becomes very familiar with everybody else, and there's a tremendous amount of comfort in that because everywhere you go everybody's going to know you.

"Horse people live and breathe horses, and for the most part it doesn't make much difference who the president is or whether there's a war going on somewhere—unless the tax code changes and there's a chance investors might buy fewer horses. But even that doesn't mean that horse people are going to do things differently. They're still going to do the same things they always do."

Best, who believes there is life after The Life, still admits that "it's hard to get out of the horse world once you're in it. To walk away from that recognition and popularity is difficult. That's why horse people get up at four in the morning and put their muddy old shoes on, their smelly old coat, and their dirty old jeans and go back out into the trenches."

Best travels in the most visible of cadres: the ranks of the grand prix jumpers. Through the miracle of ESPN and the Sports Channel, grand prix jumping reaches more spectators than anyone would have imagined twenty years ago when show jumping was an activity of which few people were aware.

Leonard A. King, Jr., president of the American Grandprix Association, believes that show jumping has succeeded "because it lends itself very well to packaging. It's roughly the same length as a football game—two to two and a half hours—which is just about the normal attention span of a spectator. And it's very simple to understand even for the nonrider. If a horse knocks a rail down, he gets four faults. If he stops, that's three faults. In addition, show jumping is conducted in an arena, where the crowd is close to the action. This, too, lends itself to television coverage."

Show jumping also features the jumpoff, a built-in overtime in which speed assumes tiebreaking importance. In the jumpoff, the horse with the fewest faults and the quickest time wins. To qualify for the jumpoff, a rider must complete the initial round(s) without incurring any faults. Yet if there are too many riders in the jumpoff, the first rounds are near meaningless. And if there are not enough riders in the jumpoff, it loses much of its suspense. The course designer is the person charged with striking the necessary balance be-

The American Gold Cup, held each fall for the benefit of the Germantown Hospital near Philadelphia, is one of the most celebrated events on the American Grandprix Association tour. At the 1990 Gold Cup, David Raposa and Seven Wonder perform before the customary sellout crowd in the Dixon Oval at the venerable Devon Horse Show grounds. This combination won the $100,000 American Invitational in Tampa, Florida, earlier in the year.

tween too much and too little of a good thing, while building courses that fit the level of competition.

"I used to build courses much differently from one location to the other," says course designer Linda Allen, a California native. "The West Coast courses were easier because there weren't as many strong riders to depend on to give you clear rounds so that there would be enough people in the jumpoff to make it interesting for the spectators. If you build to the strongest riders, eventually you'll increase the skills of the other riders, who have to improve in order to deal with the courses, but you won't get as many clear rounds as you would like to get in order to have an exciting jumpoff. Show managements on the West Coast were willing to sacrifice a little bit of crowd appeal in order to raise the standard of all riders, and the standard has come up. The courses on the coasts are equivalent now."

Courses are only as good as the horses jumping them, and as designers continue to pose more challenging questions, riders continue searching for the best four-legged answers to those questions. That search raises questions of its own: Which is the best kind of horse for show jumping? Is it possible to breed for jumping ability?

Rodney Jenkins, who began competing in shows when he was twelve and did not hang up his tack until thirty-two years later, swears by Thoroughbreds. "I really believe the best horse in the world is a Thoroughbred, if you get a good one. But you don't see them as much as you used to because racetracks are eating them alive. By the time you get them they're too crippled or too sore to do anything."

Jenkins admires the Thoroughbred's speed. "A Thoroughbred can canter faster than a warmblood can gallop." He also admires the Thoroughbred's intelligence. "Warmbloods are not real smart horses. But if a warmblood has a lot of Thoroughbred in him, he's a good horse."

Jenkins admits, however, that a Thoroughbred "is harder to get along with than a warmblood. It's much easier to take a warmblood and show him than it is to take a Thoroughbred and make him."

Jenkins also claims that "never in my wildest dreams would I try to breed a jumper. There are too many variables involved: ability, size, scope, mental attitude, heart. It's those variables that make a great jumper, not breeding."

Yet some of those variables do run in certain families, says Best. "My only exposure to breeding from a multigenerational point of view has been with the Bonn Huit line. That's where Good Twist and Gem Twist are from. That line produces a special type of horse with predictable characteristics. They're all very careful horses. They don't like to hit the jump. That has to be bred into a horse. You can't teach it. And it's something that's predominant in all the Twist horses and back further to Bonn Huit."

No matter what percentages nature and nurture contribute to the production of a good horse, Jenkins believes the horse is the dominant partner in the horse-rider affiliation. "Success is 80 percent horse and 20 percent rider," he says, "and that's giving the rider a whole lot of credit."

In pony classes the equine contribution may be

Left
More popular than the prime minister, able to leap tall oxers in an effortless bound, Canada's national treasures Ian Millar and Big Ben are crowd pleasers wherever they go. Millar of Perth, Ontario, and the 17.3-hand Belgian-bred gelding, arguably the most popular horse-and-rider combo in the world, competed at the 1992 du Maurier International Grand Prix at Spruce Meadows, Calgary. Big Ben is show jumping's all-time money winner, having earned $1.5 million plus in his career. Millar, five-time rider of the year in Canada and a member of five Canadian Olympic show-jumping teams, has won more than 100 grand prixs and jumping derbies—including the 1992 American Invitational at Tampa—a record no other rider can match.

even greater. If the grand prix jumper is the winged Pegasus of the show world, the pony is its foot soldier. Virtually all but the most late-blooming riders started out on ponies, and virtually all ponies are Welsh or some derivative thereof, obtained through a cross to a Thoroughbred, an Arabian or, sometimes, a Quarter Horse.

Ponies come in three sizes: small, 12.2 hands and under; medium, which are over 12.2 hands but no more than 13.2; and large, which are over 13.2 but no more than 14.2. Sharyn Cole, who has trained ponies and pony riders for nearly thirty years, says that ponies should have "a nice head, big eyes, long neck, legs that come square out of the body and a nice, rounded rump."

Above all ponies should be of cheerful and forgiving disposition, because during their show ring careers, which generally begin when they are four or five, they may be asked to carry five or six different riders. "A child spends an average of two years with a pony," says Cole. "Then the child outgrows the pony, physically or abilitywise, and moves on to the next size pony."

The pony, meanwhile, is sold to another developing talent and is required to adjust to a new home and new rider. The ponies most likely to make that adjustment, says Cole, "are Welsh or Welsh-Thoroughbred crosses. Sometimes Arabian crosses are a little tough to deal with. They're not as tolerant of children's mistakes."

Young riders compete on ponies in various divisions and classes. In pony hunter divisions on the "A," "B" and "C" circuits, riders try to qualify for year-end competitions in Harrisburg, Washington and the Meadowlands. In the children's hunter divisions, riders can qualify for a zone (regional) final in their own areas. There is a green pony division for ponies in their first year of showing. There is Pony Club competition. And ponies are being used even for dressage these days.

Classes within the three pony divisions include model classes, in which ponies are judged on conformation and movement, and under saddle classes, in which ponies are judged on movement at the walk, trot and canter. Ponies also may compete in three or four jumping classes. One of those classes is judged 75–25, performance vis-à-vis conformation. Small ponies jump 2'3" fences, medium ponies jump 2'6" fences, large ponies jump 3' fences.

The pony is crucial to the education of the young rider. If the chemistry between pony and child is right, if their personalities mesh, if the child looks good on a pony, and, especially, if the pony has carried a previous rider to a big win, the pony is a pearl of great price.

"You're supposed to be in it for the fun," says Cole, "but winning is fun, too. Especially from the parents' point of view after they've spent a good deal of money for a pony."

One pony class not found in show programs is the parents' class. More a club than a class, actually, the parents' contingent meets at ringside or in the grandstand at various show locations from one weekend to another during the season. Bob and Lana Ellington of Lebanon, New Jersey, were card-carrying, dues-paying, trailer-driving members of the parents' class from 1979 to 1985. Their membership began when their daughter, Carrie, started riding at the age of seven on a green pony named Yes I Can in the Short Stirrup division.

"You know how little girls are with ponies," says Lana Ellington. "Carrie asked if she could take a few lessons, and it just blossomed from there."

Four years later Yes I Can was the National Small Pony Champion. That same year, 1983, Carrie's other pony, Virginia Reel, was the Green Small-Medium Pony National Champion. Two years after that Carrie rode The Executive to a National Large Pony championship.

"We met the parents of a lot of other competitors on the circuit," says Lana Ellington. "Eventually you become like a big family, sitting together at the shows and socializing afterward."

During the years Carrie was campaigning her ponies, the Ellingtons went to thirty or forty shows annually. Asked if all that traveling and time away from home interfered with keeping the house clean and paying the bills on time, Lana Ellington replies, "Luckily, I didn't have to work at the time, so it wasn't as bad as it could have been."

And their civilian friends? "It was hard for them to understand. One time my sister told me, 'You've got to get your priorities straight.'

If this horse looks familiar, perhaps it is because you have seen the model of him produced by the Breyer toy manufacturer. Budweiser Gem Twist, three-time American Grandprix Association Horse of the Year, who is the second-leading all-time money winner on that circuit, and Greg Best, AGA's Rookie of the Year in 1987, were for many years the country's most recognizable horse-and-rider combination.

Darren Graziano and Grandessa tackle the second part of a combination in a junior jumper class at the 1990 I Love New York horse show in Lake Placid, New York. Located in the Adirondack Mountains, Lake Placid is the site of several weeks of competition each summer.

"At first we did worry that Carrie might miss out on activities at school, but if she wanted to do something with her friends, she did. For example, when a class at one of the big shows was scheduled for the same day as a prom, she skipped the class to go to the prom and went to the show the next day."

The Ellingtons graduated to the junior parents' class when Carrie moved up to junior hunters and jumpers. Now that she's at Boston University, riding in grand prixs on weekends and during the summer, they watch her career from a greater distance.

"We were lucky because Carrie always made her animals worth more than they were when she got them," says Lana Ellington. "Selling them at a profit helped to pay for a lot of expenses. If she hadn't done that, she couldn't have shown as much as she did."

When the Ellingtons found that grand prix horses were beyond the family budget, Carrie worked with her junior jumper, a Dutch Warmblood named Zoef, and made him into a grand prix horse. She won the first welcome stake at the Winter Equestrian Festival

Jumper riders may compete informally, i.e., without their coats, in events below the grand prix level. Farley Dixon in his shirtsleeves rides Legend in a preliminary jumper class during Desert Circuit II in Indio, California. The preliminary class is where horses take their first steps toward grand prix and open jumper events.

in 1993 and rode in the American Invitational in Tampa that year.

The cost of being well or even decently mounted is the first obstacle a beginning rider must jump. For every family that cannot afford a made horse, there are hundreds of others that cannot afford a horse at all.

"Unfortunately, it is very difficult for somebody of limited means to make it in our business," says trainer Leo Conroy. "However, it's not impossible. The best advice I can give to people who cannot afford a horse or many lessons is to hook up with a good, name professional in any capacity—groom, working student, whatever—and to show by their initiative that they are serious and dedicated and really want to get ahead. Top riders aren't going to hire people with no experience to be their head groom at Devon, but they

will probably be able to find a niche for them at the farm." Conroy emphasizes "top trainers and riders" because he believes that "one lesson a month from a top professional is worth more than ten lessons a month from someone who is mediocre."

Not everybody aspires to a career in horses. Some young people simply want to take part in a few shows because they have a friend who does and it sounds interesting.

"The smaller, unrecognized horse shows are thriv-

Right
Like fighters pacing about in their robes before a fight, three horses wearing coolers are walked by their grooms— while a fourth horse is limbered up—before competing at the 1991 Winter Equestrian Festival at the Palm Beach Polo and Equestrian Club.

Katie Monahan Prudent of Middleburg, Virginia, and Silver Skates put in a heads-up performance at the Michelob fence during the $40,000 Michelob Upperville Jumper Classic at the 1991 Upperville Colt and Horse Show. Prudent, who reports that she learned to ride before she learned to read, won the American Horse Shows Association Medal and the ASPCA Maclay equitation championships as a young rider. She has also been the American Grandprix Association's Rider of the Year on three occasions and has ridden three different horses to horse of the year honors.

ing," says Conroy, "and a lot of stables cater to that clientele. The person looking to compete in horse shows as a hobby would go to a local stable looking to work in exchange for lessons."

Margie Goldstein, two-time American Grandprix Association Rider of the Year, used a similar approach to get extra lessons and horses to ride when she was not yet in her teens. "My parents could afford one lesson a week," says Goldstein. "We weren't paupers, but I'm the youngest of three children, and my parents were putting my brothers through school.

"I worked odd jobs until I was thirteen, then I started working at Gladewinds Farm in Florida. I did grooming, tacking up horses and so forth. I did the

dog and cat kennels. Anything I could do. They paid me in lessons or rides. Work so many hours, get an extra lesson. I never had the money to train with high-profile trainers, but I did take clinics whenever I could."

The association between student and trainer is much like an apprenticeship, and the lessons absorbed around the barn are lessons that are valuable throughout life. Character as well as careers are molded in the training processes.

The trainer who has influenced more young riders in this country is George Morris, who virtually invented hunter seat equitation, in which a rider is judged on correctness of position, accuracy and style.

Left
Frenchman Henri Prudent and Fair Lady IV during the $35,000 American Banker's Insurance Internationale Cup, a 1994 World Cup Qualifier, held at West Palm Beach, Florida. A former three-day event rider in Europe, Prudent is married to show-jumping legend Katie Monahan. They operate Plain Bay Farm in Middleburg, Virginia, to which they have imported and trained many successful show jumpers.

At the age of twenty-two, with the horse world at his feet, Morris left riding to study acting for seventeen months at the Neighborhood Playhouse Theater school in New York City. After deciding that he was "a working but not a brilliant actor," Morris returned to The Life and began teaching in 1964. During the next twenty years, twenty of his students won the American Horse Shows Association's Medal, the ASPCA Maclay, or both.

Morris arrived at shows like the commander of an invasion force, his charges occupying as many as seventy stalls. "It was all but assured," says a former pupil, "that one of George's students would win any given event at a show."

More important than the ribbons are the values that Morris and other teachers impart to their pupils. "Riding with me is very good for young people," says Morris. "I instill discipline. I instill motivation. And I instill a work ethic. I'm sure all of those things carry on outside the ring."

Stories about Morris are part of horse show lore. Most of them turn on a his-way-or-no-way theme. "I was fifteen when I started riding with George," recalls a former student, who says that she was more anxious waiting to hear if she would get to ride with Morris than she was waiting to find out if she had gotten into college. "One of the first times George saw me he said that I needed to shut up, dress a lot better and pay more attention to what I was doing. He was absolutely right."

"Discipline has to do with stable management. It has to do with cleanliness, tidiness, spit-and-polish," says Morris. "It has to do with riding apparel. It has to be very, very fixed. I've always found that the disciplined approach works best in my teaching. Ultimately, discipline and structure allow people to succeed on their own and to become excellent."

Three thousand miles west of Hunterdon, Morris's hundred-acre farm in northern New Jersey, is the Flintridge Riding Club at the base of Flint Canyon in California. While Morris was conquering the East

Coast, a West Coast trainer named Jimmy Williams, who had also done a stint in acting, was working on his own legend. In 1960, the year Morris rode on the United States Equestrian Team's Olympic show jumping team, Williams was named Horseman of the Year by the American Horse Shows Association (AHSA). Seventeen years later he was named Horseman of the Year by the California Professional Horsemen's Association. In 1990, at the age of seventy-three, he was inducted into the Show Jumping Hall of Fame.

Williams's students have won virtually every major hunter or jumper competition on the West Coast. Hap Hansen, Rob Gage and Susan Hutchison all trained with Williams and all have been American Grandprix Association Rider of the Year.

When Williams began training, the sun rose in the east and stayed there as far as the horse show world was concerned. West Coast riders looking for a place in the sun came east to train and—in many cases—to live. That eastward migration still occurs, but to a far lesser extent than it once did. In time, it may not occur at all.

If California is going to achieve parity with the east, there must be a sufficient base of competitive opportunities in which California riders can develop their skills. That foundation is now in place.

During the 1980s, the number of California shows sanctioned by the American Horse Shows Association leaped from 178 to 346, an increase of 94 percent. In 1990 California had the largest growth in AHSA-recognized shows of any state in the Union.

The Pacific Coast Horse Shows Association (PCHA), most of whose gatherings are AHSA sanctioned, scheduled fifty-three A-rated hunter-jumper shows in California in 1992. The majority were held in Southern California, south of Santa Barbara and west of the San Andreas fault, a 25,000-square-mile area about the size of West Virginia.

According to Linda Allen, one reason for all that growth is the weather. "It's possible to run horse shows virtually all year around in good conditions

Looking like townspeople surveying the field where the space ship landed, riders and trainers walk the course before a jumper class at the 1991 Winter Equestrian Festival in West Palm Beach, Florida. As they walk, they measure distances between jumps, see how securely the rails of the jumps nestle in their cups and formulate a strategy for riding the course.

with only the odd show getting rained out. You don't have to ride in a freezing, indoor icebox of an arena all winter.

"But the biggest difference between California and other places is the atmosphere. California is more laid back. It's a friendlier, less complicated place to compete and, in many ways, to live. Many of us consider the climate, the showing conditions and the living conditions better in California than they are anywhere else."

While many Californians were heading east to ride, there was a small but influential migration in the opposite direction. Two of the most notable transplanted easterners are Victor Hugo-Vidal and Karen Healey. Hugo-Vidal—founder of Cedar Lodge Farm in Stamford, Connecticut, coach of Medal winners James Hulick and Brooke Hodgson and AHSA Horseman of the Year in 1971—moved to Southern California in December 1978. Three years later Karen Healey, a successful junior rider who had worked for four and a half years at Hunterdon, arrived in California. In 1991 Hugo-Vidal and Healey were the California Professional Horsemen's Association Horseman and Horsewoman of the Year.

Another easterner now hanging his tack in California is Bernie Traurig, a triple-threat rider who has won more than thirty grand prix show jumping events and fifteen grand prixs and grand prix special classes in dressage, and who qualified for the Olympic three-day team in 1964 but withdrew after his horse was injured. Traurig is based at Ziyad Abdul-Jawar's Albert Court training center in Rancho Sante Fe.

Healey recalls that when she moved to California in 1981, "people had one horse to do the hunters, the equitation, and the jumpers. The concept of having a second equitation horse was unheard of. I knew I had made the right move, though, because Californians were ready to go on and do. I thought it was possible to work out of California without making the trip to Mecca and to be competitive with the right preparation and the right horses."

She was correct. By the mid-1980s, says Healey, "California juniors had begun to make an impact in the East. I've had kids in the top ten in the Medal and the Maclay finals consistently since the mid-1980s."

Although California's "climate and atmosphere are wonderful," says Allen, "in some ways they're a bit of a detriment. There isn't quite as strong a work ethic yet in California as there is in the East. That often makes the level of competition higher on the East Coast.

"If I arrive at the schooling area at six-fifteen in the morning at an East Coast show, just about every professional and all the serious amateurs and juniors will be on a horse. Many of them on their second or third horses. In California I might see one or two people riding and a few grooms longeing horses."

California hosted the Olympics in 1984 and the World Cup in 1992. It is also now the permanent home of the Desert Circuit: six weeks of showing and six grand prixs at the Empire Polo Club and Equestrian Center in Indio. The six grand prixs, the jewels in the Desert Circuit's crown, are complemented by a full slate of showing. About 175 classes are offered at each show, with competition taking place in five rings simultaneously, except on Sundays, when the grand prixs are the centers of attention.

The Desert Circuit, which runs from late January to mid-March, with a week off following the first three weeks, is produced by Horse Shows in the Sun (HITS). "We're going to offer as much in the long run as Palm Beach does," says Tony Hitchcock, one of the organizers of this circuit. "The show facility is in the middle of the Palm Springs winter resort area, which provides access to the rich and beautiful and famous just as much as do Palm Beach in Florida and the Hamptons in New York."

Portions of the Desert Circuit, namely some of its grand prix events, were previously held in Goodyear, Arizona. HITS elected to focus its activities on Indio, says Hitchcock, "because of the address. If you tell sponsors you're going to position their products in Palm Springs, that's quite different from positioning them in Goodyear, Arizona. Big events need to be conducted in places like Palm Springs, where owners are happy relaxing and where sponsors will see a big audience."

Hitchcock, who is also the co-executive director of

The Hampton Classic Horse Show, says that HITS "expects, over a period of years, to create a Hampton Classic ambience in Indio. There's a lot of time during a show week when your horse isn't going, and it's nice to be able to walk out of your hotel door onto one of the best golf courses in the United States. That's a powerfully seductive force for owners."

Even more seductive is watching your horse compete. But, says Michael Golden of Chester, New Jersey, the owner of Gem Twist, "it is not enjoyable. I guess it's a paradox. It's enjoyable in one sense, but it's also nerve-racking. In fact, it's the most anxiety-creating condition I go through. There isn't a fence that Gem takes that I don't take with him."

Golden prefers to take his fences in a quiet part of the arena, away from the people with whom he has come to a show. At one competition in Madison Square Garden, Golden slipped away to a private spot to watch Gem Twist in the Mercedes Grandprix. The spot Golden chose was already occupied by Frank Chapot, the horse's trainer.

"If you had looked at us while Gem was going," says Golden, "you would have thought we were doing some kind of break dance. I don't know if there's an owner who doesn't go through the same anxiety."

Although grand prix jumping captures most of the headlines, hunter competition is still thriving and evolving. "There are a lot of new avenues for showing hunters today," says Don Stewart, a hunter trainer based in Ocala, Florida. The broadest of those avenues is the World Hunter Championship show in Louisville, Kentucky.

Like the grand prix courses, hunter courses are much more technical than they were twenty-five years ago, says Stewart. "In addition, there's a big market for the three-foot hunter now. That's a highly competitive division for people who are not interested in competing at the 3'6" level. I think the new World Champion Hunter Rider Foundation will also give everybody a chance to do some different things also."

Right
Was it the deep footing through this combination or the 12 faults on the scoreboard that elicited the grimace from Rich Fellers? An Oregon native who is based now in Diamond Bar, California, Fellers competed on Va Voom, a 15.2-hand Thoroughbred-Trakehner cross mare, at the duMaurier International Grand Prix at the 1992 "Masters" in Spruce Meadows, Calgary.

This horse and rider in the amateur owner jumper class at the Florida Winter Equestrian Festival personify two of the cardinal rules of show jumping: be clear and be fast.

No matter what the class or what the competition, show horses are among the world's finest athletes. When the best ones walk into the ring and sense the crowd is watching, they seem to grow in size. Their chests swell, their eyes get big, their ears come forward, they turn into The Incredible Equine. Two hours ago, back in their stalls, they might have had a puppy face on, fooling around or giving the groom a hassle. But when it comes time to go into the ring, they become entirely focused and eager to get to work.

Those special horses are as remarkable as they are unforgettable. Electricity crackles when they enter the arena, and more than one spectator is thinking. "I'm glad I'm here to see this, because this is really special."

Susan Hutchison of Flintridge, California, the 1992 American Grandprix Association Rider of the Year, began riding with the fabled California trainer Jimmy Williams when she was five. At the 1993 Desert Circuit, held in Indio, California, Hutchison and ASAP compete in the $30,000 La Quinta Classic Grand Prix. Later during that circuit they returned to win the $100,000 Crown Royal Grandprix.

Something Special and Rob Gage of Burbank, California, during the jumpoff of the $30,000 La Quinta Classic Grand Prix at the 1993 Desert Circuit, Indio, California. In 1985 Gage became the first West Coast rider to win the Mercedes Rider of the Year title. By the end of 1991, he was ninth on the American Grandprix Association's all-time-money-winner's list.

Left
Virginia's Rodney Jenkins and Heisman in a grand prix at the 1988 Old Salem Farm Horse Show in New York. Jenkins, who retired the following year, was a rider cast in a supernatural mold with the instincts of a heat-seeking missile and the hands of a safecracker. When he was twenty-two, he won the first of his five leading rider titles at Devon. Two decades later, his skills undiminished, he was the American Grandprix Association's Rider of the Year, the American Horse Shows Association's Horseman of the Year, and a double silver medalist in the Pan-American Games. He won seventy-eight grand prixs, a fifth of those after he had turned forty. He won the American Gold Cup five times, four of them in a row. Those who saw Jenkins in his prime—which lasted longer than many people's careers—say that we may never see his like again.

His eye for a horse and rider as keen as ever, former show jumping great Rodney Jenkins of Montpelier Station, Virginia, judges the United States Equestrian Team Medal Finals.

A junior rider clears the water jump at the United States Equestrian Team Medal Finals in Gladstone, New Jersey. Riders must qualify at horse shows during the year in order to compete in two Medal finals, one on the East Coast, the other on the West Coast. Contestants are judged on form, control and accuracy during three phases of competition: on the flat, gymnastics and jumping. On the last day of competition, the top four riders switch horses before jumping a shortened course. Winning the USET Medal is a definitive accomplishment for a young rider.

New Jersey's Nicole Shahinian and Moonstruck compete in the 1991 Junior Amateur Jumper Classic at the Winter Equestrian Festival. Shahinian finished her junior career in 1992 by winning the Maclay championship at the National Horse Show. In 1991 she was awarded the gold medal in show jumping at the Young Riders Championships. She now rides professionally in both hunter and jumper classes.

Right
On the august grounds of the United States Equestrian Team's headquarters in Gladstone, New Jersey—North America's equestrian mecca—a young aspirant to the USET Medal (East Coast version) watches the action while her horse nods out irreverently.

Susan Hostnick and Riviera City in the Junior Amateur Owner Jumper Classic at the 1990 Ox Ridge Charity Horse Show held at the Ox Ridge Hunt Club in Darien, Connecticut. Riviera City was the 1989 American Horse Shows Association's Horse of the Year in the amateur owner jumper division, in which horses must be owned by their riders or a member of the riders' immediate families.

Right
Carrie Ellington of Lebanon, New Jersey, and Zoef are the centerpiece of an artfully landscaped jump at the 1990 United States Equestrian Team Talent Derby, held at the Hampton Classic on Long Island. The Talent Derby, a jumper class for riders twenty-five or younger, was designed to help identify riders who might represent the USET in international competition. Ellington, a pre-law student at Boston University, and Zoef placed sixth in this event. They now compete on the grand prix circuit.

While Michelle Blair checks the oil and cleans the windshield, Megan Braid of Unionville, Pennsylvania, sits quietly on her pony, Hosanna, before a pony hunter class at the 1991 Winter Equestrian Festival.

Right
Just as horses are, ponies are judged on manners, jumping style and consistency as their lilliputian riders guide them over a course dotted with 2'3" jumps. Margaret Jayne and Space Invader competed in a small pony hunter class at the 1991 Winter Equestrian Festival.

Julia McGeoch from Greenwich, Connecticut, and Silver Edition compete in a Pony Medal class, an equitation class for pony riders, at the 1992 Ox Ridge Charity Horse Show.

Abigail Vietor of New York City scrutinizes the other riders in pony hunter rounds at the 1991 Winter Equestrian Festival at the Palm Beach Polo and Equestrian Club. Later in the day Vietor will compete in large pony hunter classes.

A big smile on a little rider, Jennifer Dermody by name, before a short stirrup class at the Gill St. Bernard's Horse Show in Gladstone.

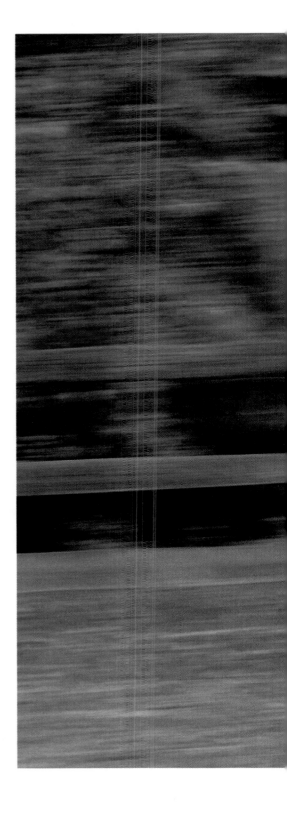

For many riders the thousand-mile journey to the grand prix level begins with a few steps at the walk, trot and canter in short stirrup classes. At the Gill St. Bernard's Horse Show in Gladstone, New Jersey, this rider and her pony take their first steps while getting their feet wet at the lowest equitation level.

With power, speed and agility, this horse and rider rocket over an oxer at the 1991 Ox Ridge Charity Horse Show.

Who would have thought that rock star John Cougar Mellencamp would have a daughter competing in horse shows in West Palm Beach, Florida? Teddi Jo Mellencamp seems to like the idea as she heads toward a pony hunter class at the Winter Equestrian Festival.

The Upperville Colt and Horse Show, held at the Grafton Farm show grounds in Virginia hunt country, is the oldest and most eminent horse show in the United States. In 1991, at the 138th Upperville gathering, Randy DeWitt shows Sultan's Holiday, owned by Tim Gulick, in a Thoroughbred breeding class.

Right
The 1992 American Horse Shows Association's National Reserve Champions in the regular conformat on hunter division were Don Stewart and Western Prospect. Stewart, whose business is based in Ocala, Florida, rode Western Prospect in a regular conformation hunter class at the 1993 Winter Equestrian Festival. Stewart is a respected professional who rides, trains and judges hunters on the "A" circuit.

Barb Gould and Quantum leap over rails that look like a modern-art painting in a high amateur owner jumper class at the 1992 Greater Cincinnati Classic Horse Show. The GCCHS, an important stop on the Midwest summer "A" circuit, is held on the infield at Turfway Park in Florence, Kentucky.

Right
The horse showing season on the East Coast begins with the Winter Equestrian Festival at the Palm Beach Polo and Equestrian Club. There, horses and riders spend several months getting back into the saddle before moving across the state to Tampa. At the 1993 festival in Palm Beach, Michael Matz rides Big Spender in a high-preliminary jumper class.

Formally attired in the requisite shadbelly and top hat, Vera Sapp rides Strategy in the Junior Amateur Hunter Classic at the 1993 Desert Circuit II in Indio, California. This two-round hunter class is often held on the last day of competition at "A" shows.

Left
Keeping her eye on the next class, Keri Stout, a young rider from Alabama, hands the ribbon from her last class to her trainer at the 1990 Hampton Classic on Long Island. One of the largest and most popular stops on the East Coast circuit, the Hampton Classic attracts more than 1,000 horses to its "A"-rated hunter and jumper divisions.

Peter Wylde and Twilight in a regular conformation hunter class at the 1993 Winter Equestrian Festival. Hunters are judged on their way of going, pace, jumping style and manners. Hunter classes were designed originally to determine a horse's suitability for the hunt field. They have evolved into something quite different, but the rider's goal is still a smooth, comfortable ride.

The United States Equestrian Team Festival of Champions, held annually at team headquarters in Gladstone, New Jersey, is a week-long event featuring show jumping, dressage and combined driving competition. The USET Talent Derby, a jumper class for riders below the age of twenty-five, is part of the festival. The winners of the 1991 derby were Schuyler Riley and Flamingo.

Entrant 226 and friend stand on the line in a green conformation model class at the 1991 Winter Equestrian Festival in West Palm Beach, Florida. Like contestants in a beauty pageant, horses in a model class are judged on their physical attributes and way of moving.

Right
In equitation classes a rider is judged on correctness of position, accuracy and style. Lauren Hough of Morgan Hill, California, appears to be three for three over this fence in a United States Equestrian Team Medal Equitation Class at Desert Circuit II in Indio, California. Hough, a top junior competitor, also rides hunters and jumpers.

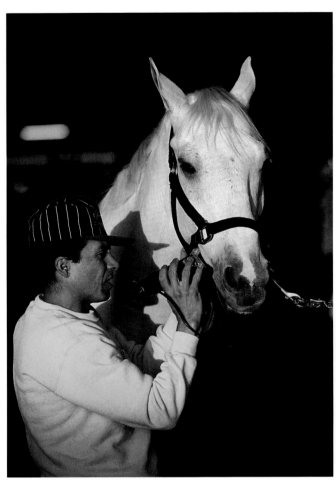

The junior jumper Money Man gets an early-morning facial from Mario Diaz at the Centennial Farm stalls at the Palm Beach Polo and Equestrian Club.

Home is where the potted plants and the farm sign are. During the Florida circuit each winter, horses, their riders and their attendants spend as many as three months at the Palm Beach Polo and Equestrian Club in West Palm Beach. The permanent stables and the personal touches make this home away from home more homelike.

At the 1992 United States Equestrian Team Festival of Champions, the final selection trial for the Barcelona Olympics, Norman Dello Joio and Irish, owned by Windsome Farm, secured their spot on the team. Dello Joio, sometimes called "Stormin' Norman," is the son of the Pulitzer Prize- and Emmy-winning composer of the same name. Dello Joio the younger is a veteran USET rider. In 1983 he won the FEI World Cup in Vienna, Austria, and the duMaurier Ltd. at the "Masters" in Spruce Meadows.

Right
Hugh Mutch and S&L Ballet hit the bricks, figuratively, during the $30,000 La Quinta Classic Grand Prix at the 1993 Desert Circuit, Indio, California. The son of Ronnie Mutch, a well-known East Coast trainer, "Bert" was a successful junior rider before going to work for Sam and Libby Edleman, longtime show jumping enthusiasts, owners and sponsors.

Overleaf
Spruce Meadows in Calgary, Alberta, is North America's finest equestrian facility. This opulent complex, built in 1976, is the site of several major competitions each year. At the 1992 Western Gas Marketing "Western Welcome," Jennifer Foster of Brampton, Ontario, guides Zeus over a triple bar jump. Foster was a member of the Canadian Equestrian Team at the Barcelona Olympics.

Alain Vaillancourt and Balderdash during the 1993 Desert Circuit in Indio, California, the date capital of the nation. Vaillancourt began riding in his native Canada in 1966. He now lives in San Juan Capistrano, California, where he rides at The Oaks for Joan Irvine Smith, a former show rider who now owns numerous jumpers.

If the shoe fits, the farrier made it. Farriers combine old-world muscle with newfangled equipment like the propane forge, electric welder and electric shoe-tapping guns. Joe Johnson of Winchester, Virginia, hammers out a living attending to the needs of international riders and their horses in North America and Europe.

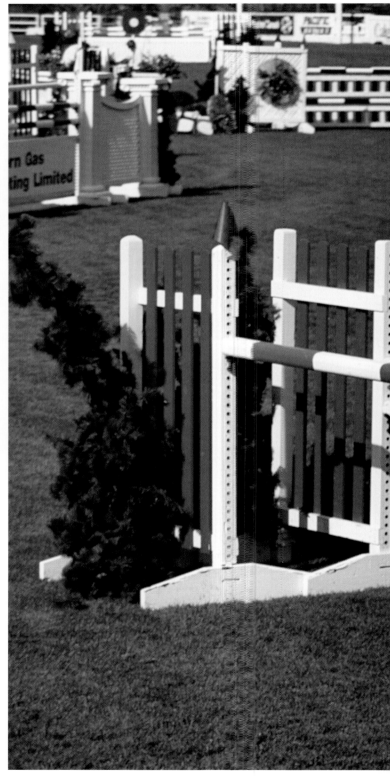

Two members of Lord Strathcona's Horse "Royal Canadians" sit at attention as the official color guards of the "Masters" at Spruce Meadows, Calgary.

Canadian Mark Laskin, who rides with Pinon Farm in Sante Fe, New Mexico, and Sullivan competing in the Western Gas Marketing "Western Welcome" at the "Masters" in Spruce Meadows, Calgary. Show jumping, which does not have to buck as much competition from other sports in Canada as it does in the United States, is more popular north of the border and is, therefore, able to attract more major corporations as sponsors.

Not one to mince words or expressions, George Morris contemplates one of his students in the schooling ring.

George Morris and Zanzibar at the 1990 American Gold Cup in Devon, Pennsylvania. A peerless teacher, ageless competitor and consummate horseman, Morris has been in the ribbons during each of the last five decades. He was the youngest rider, at fourteen, to win the American Horse Shows Association Medal and the ASPCA Maclay finals in the same year. He has ridden on a United States Equestrian Team silver medal–winning Olympic show jumping squad. He wrote the best-selling Hunter Seat Equitation. *And he wrote the book on training equitation and grand prix jumper riders.*

Adult jumper classes, conceived by horse show promoter Tom Struzzieri, became the Adult Jumper League with the sponsorship of horse-and-farm insurers Marshall & Sterling. The purpose of the league is to provide a competitive venue for riders who are not quite ready for the amateur owner jumper class. Tracey Lowery rides Allan Shore's Dutch Warmblood Constantyjn in an adult jumper class at the 1992 Hartwood Show Jumping Festival in Pittsburgh, Pennsylvania. The finals of the Adult Jumper League, where the maximum fence height is 3'6", are held at the Washington International Horse Show. Lowery finished first in the 1992 league final aboard Juke Box Johnny and ninth on Constantyjn.

Debbie Stephens of Ambler, Pennsylvania, formerly Debbie Shaffner, has been a star on the grand prix circuit for many years. Stephens, who married course designer Steve Stephens, competed on La Just Valeur at the 1991 American Bankers Grandprix in West Palm Beach, Florida. A competitor at the national level since she was ten, Stephens won the $100,000 American Invitational on Volan in 1993.

Since winning the Maclay at the age of fifteen, Leslie Lenehan has been a world-class rider and trainer for more than two decades. In late 1992, a twist of fate brought two great talents together, when Leslie rode Gem Twist to Horse of the Year honors. At the 1994 Winter Equestrian Festival in West Palm Beach, Florida, Leslie and Gem Twist clear the final oxer on their way to winning the $125,000 Budweiser/AGA Championship.

When Lisa Jacquin bought a young ex-racehorse as a jumper prospect, she named him For The Moment because that was how long she expected to have him. More than ten years later Jacquin and "Fred" won this qualifying class for the $50,000 United States Equestrian Team Show Jumping Championship Grandprix at the 1991 Festival of Champions in Gladstone, New Jersey. Two days later, under a heavy rain, they won the final of this event. For The Moment, a horse for all moments, is the all-time money-winning jumper in the United States and was the Cartier/American Grandprix Association's Horse of the Year in 1991.

The water jump, which can measure 12 to 14 feet from front to back, often presents the greatest challenge of all the ob-stacles on a grand prix course. Many horses are wary of water, and this jumper is going to great heights not to get his feet wet in the $60,000 Crown Royal Empire State Grandprix at the 1990 Old Salem Farm horse show in Old Salem, New York.

Urstadt, party of six. On a hazy Sunday morning Jordy Urstadt, Springbok and their convoy make their way to the ring where horse and rider will compete in the Junior/Amateur Jumper Classic at the 1990 Ox Ridge Charity Horse Show in Darien, Connecticut. Attending Urstadt (from right to left) are an unidentified groom, Mary Joan Manfredi (an assistant trainer), Andre Dignelli (an assistant trainer) and Judy Richter (head trainer).

Over her country's symbol, the maple leaf, flies Jill Henselwood on Canadian Colours during the Western Gas Marketing "Western Welcome" at the 1992 "Masters" at Spruce Meadows, Calgary. Henselwood, from Juniper Farms in Oxford Mills, Ontario, trains with Ian Millar, Canada's leading jumper rider, and is riding one of Millar's former mounts in this competition. In 1992, Henselwood was the leading female rider on the Canadian circuit.

California hosted the Olympics in 1984 and the World Cup in 1992. It is also the permanent home of the premier winter circuit on the West Coast: the Desert Circuit, six weeks of hunter-jumper shows and six grand prix jumping events at the Empire Polo Club and Equestrian Center in Indio, cheek by palm by pocketbook with Palm Springs. While spectators and sponsors look on, Dale Harvey and Pik Trump II clear a triple bar jump during the $30,000 La Quinta Classic Grand Prix.

Left
An interesting contrast with the logo on this jump, John Whitaker of Great Britain and Henderson Gammon were the eventual winners of the $680,000 duMaurier International Grand Prix in 1992. The most lucrative grand prix in the world—the winner's share of the purse is $225,000— the duMaurier has been held at Spruce Meadows since 1981. Whitaker also won this event on Next Mon Santa in 1989.

Peter Leone and Crown Royal Oxo in the United States Equestrian Team Show Jumping Championship Grand Prix at the 1992 Festival of Champions at Gladstone, New Jersey. Peter, who has ridden for the USET and was a member of the winning Nation's Cup team in 1988, is also a member of "Team Leone," whose two other members are his brothers Mark and Armand, Jr. The Leones, who are sponsored by Crown Royal, ride out of their RI-ARM farm in Franklin Lakes, New Jersey.

The stylish spectator tents at the 1992 Hartwood Show Jumping Festival in Pittsburgh make a formal backdrop for David Raposa of Clinton, New York, and Top Flight during the Waterworks Mall Welcome Stake. Raposa, a three-time winner of the Rolex/United States Equestrian Team's Talent Derby, rides several jumpers in grand prix competition.

The Welcome Stake at the Greater Cincinnati Classic Horse Show is a qualifying class for the $75,000 Adrian J. French American Jumping Classic. Hoping to qualify for the latter, Todd Minikus of Lake Forest, Illinois, and Thrilling compete in the former. Minikus was the winner of the 1990 President's Cup Grandprix at the Washington International Horse Show.

People who believe that talent is heritable could cite McLain Ward as proof of that theory. The son of well-known trainer and jumper rider Barney Ward, McLain was one of the top junior competitors in the United States. He was the youngest rider, at fourteen to win the Rolex/United States Equestrian Team Show Jumping Talent Derby. Ten weeks later he became the youngest rider to win the Rolex/USET Medal Finals. On Ladybird, McLain, who was not quite sixteen, rode in a junior jumper class at the 1990 I Love New York show in Lake Placid. The following year he was the American Grandprix Association's Rolex Rookie of the Year.

Michael Dorman, a New Yorker who now rides out of New Hope, Pennsylvania, and the intermediate jumper Beaucoup at the 1993 Winter Equestrian Festival at the Palm Beach Polo and Equestrian Club. Beaucoup is one of several jumpers being developed by Dorman, who is a consistent competitor in grand prix jumper contests.

Quiet, calm and majestic as their shadows, a horse and rider reflect on the coming competition in a grand prix jumping class at the 1991 Winter Equestrian Festival in West Palm Beach.

Canadian-born Mario Deslauriers, who now resides in Culpepper, Virginia, returned to Canada to compete in the 1992 "Masters" on Scirocco at Spruce Meadows in Calgary. Deslauriers' first riding instructor was his father, Roger, who operated the Bromont Equestrian Centre, site of the equestrian events for the 1976 Olympics. In 1984, at the age of nineteen, Deslauriers, riding Aramis, became the first Canadian to win the FEI (Fédération Equestre International) World Cup. He also has ridden twice for the Canadian Equestrian Team.

Left
Tim Grubb of Whitehouse, New Jersey, and Denizen, a 17-hand Hanoveran gelding, at the 1992 "Masters" at Spruce Meadow, Calgary. Born in Leicestershire, England, Grubb has lived in the United States for several years and is now a U.S. citizen. While still a British citizen, he represented England on Denizen at the 1992 Olympics and was a member of the silver medal-winning British show jumping team at the 1984 Olympics.

Hap Hansen of Rancho Mirage, California, and Accord at the 1993 Desert Circuit, Indio, California. The 1990 Johnny Walker/American Grandprix Association Rider of the Year—and one of the all-time leading money winners on the AGA circuit—Hansen has ridden several times in Europe as a member of the United States Equestrian Team. Like fellow Californians Hutchinson and Gage, Hansen also trained with the late Jimmy Williams.

Left
The General and Michael Matz in the $125,000 Budweiser/ AGA Championship at the 1994 Winter Equestrian Festival in West Palm Beach, Florida. The all-time leading money winner in the American Grandprix Association, Matz, of Collegeville, Pennsylvania, is a four-time winner of the United States Equestrian Team's Show Jumping Championship. In addition to representing the United States in the 1976 and 1992 Olympics, Matz also has won six Pan-American Games medals, including the gold, and was the 1981 Volvo World Cup Champion.

Riding the corporate-sponsored Crown Royal Artos, Mark Leone of Franklin Lakes, New Jersey, competes at the 1992 Hartwood Show Jumping Festival in Pittsburgh, Pennsylvania. The youngest of three brothers who are all talented grand prix riders, Mark has been competing successfully at the grand prix level since 1981. He was the United States Equestrian Team's Young Rider of the Year in 1982.

Linda Southern-Heathcott and Plymouth Voyager cruise over the Grain Elevator jump at the 1992 Bechtel "Welcome" Open at Spruce Meadows, Calgary. The first corporate-sponsored show jumper in Canada, Southern-Heathcott is the daughter of Ron and Marge Southern, who own and operate the splendid Spruce Meadows facility, the venue for fifty major show-jumping competitions between 1976 and 1992.

Margie Goldstein and Aristo are escorted over the Sea World jump by Shamu (left) and Shamette (right) during the $40,000 Michelob Upperville Jumper Classic at the 1991 Upperville Colt and Horse Show. During the last decade sponsorship of equestrian events increased significantly, and by the end of the decade some corporations began subsidizing individual horses, a custom long established in Europe.

Life imitates a tack-shop display window in this vignette from the Upperville Colt and Horse Show.

Judge, trainer, course designer, two-time Olympic medalist and world-class grand prix rider Joe Fargis has been a presence in the horse-show world for many years. Fargis, competing on Cordane in an intermediate jumper class at the 1993 Winter Equestrian Festival, operates Sandron Farm training center with his partner and fellow Olympian Conrad Homfeld in Southampton, New York, and West Palm Beach, Florida.

Horse-show photographer James Leslie Parker in the pink cap managed to get Heather Lloyd of Mahwah, New Jersey, and West Palm Beach, Florida, to smile after winning the Junior Amateur Hunter Classic at the 1990 Ox Ridge Charity Horse Show Lloyd's horse, Killer Tom, however, seemed to be practicing what is known in intelligence circles as a thousand-yard stare.

Right
Puissance classes are dedicated to the proposition that horses can fly. Beezie Patton of Cazenovia, New York, and Ping Pong test this theory during the $10,000 Puissance Stake at the 1992 National Horse Show at the Meadowlands in New Jersey. Patton, the leading international rider at the show, finished second in the puissance to Terry Rudd and Alf. Eleven riders started this class, where the jumping height began at 6'0". For the second round of competition the wall was built up to 6'5". For the third and final round the height was 6'8".

Overleaf
Margie Goldstein and Aristo gallop on course during the $50,000 Grand Prix of New York at the 1992 National Horse
Show in the Meadowlands Arena, East Rutherford, New Jersey. Before moving to New Jersey in 1989, the National had
spent the first 105 years of its life in Madison Square Garden. The National is part of the end-of-the-season indoor circuit,
whose other stops include Harrisburg and Washington before the National and the Royal Winter Fair in Toronto after it.

DRESSAGE

A universal training regimen, a competitive discipline and a state of mind—this is dressage. Zen and the art of horsemanship. Elegant concentration. Horse and rider tracing a meticulous progression of circles, serpentines, zigzags, and lateral movements in which the horse appears to dance of its own volition.

Dressage is at once the most ancient equestrian exercise in the world and the latest show ring vogue in late-twentieth-century America. The basic philosophy of dressage—"anything forced and misunderstood can never be beautiful"—was expressed for the first time more than 2,300 years ago in Greece, where the systematic training of horses was both an artistic accomplishment and a means of ensuring that cavalry mounts could be controlled with one hand during battle.

In the latter, practical, sense dressage is as meaningful to all riders today as it was to the cavalry in ancient Greece. "Every horse begins with the same basic training, whether he's a jumper, a cross-country horse, a dressage horse or a pleasure horse," says Lendon Gray, two-time Olympian and winner of more national championships, nearly thirty, than any other U.S. rider. "All horses must learn to respond to the rider's aids, and this is dressage whether you call it that or not."

In the artistic sense, competitive dressage with a capital D is a fast-growing phenomenon in this country. Between 1980 and 1990 the number of competitions sanctioned jointly by the United States Dressage Federation (USDF) and the American Horse Shows Association grew from 206 to 531 annually, and individual membership in the USDF grew from 8,832 to 21,605. Riders can participate in dressage at ten different levels according to their own and their horses' capabilities. Competition begins at the training level and becomes increasingly more challenging through first, second, third, fourth, and fifth levels, Prix St. Georges, Intermediate I and II and Grand Prix.

"People are discovering that it is very rewarding to train a horse through the levels of dressage with the aim of developing it into a top-class performer," says Fiona Baan, director of dressage and driving for the United States Equestrian Team. "They are also learn-

Left
Betsy Steiner of Sherrard, Illinois, and Magari exhibiting excellent flexion and bending in a fourth-level test at the 1993 Southern Comfort Dressage held at Clarcona Horseman's Park. Steiner rode on the USET's 1990 World Championship team, the 1991 bronze medal–winning Olympic sports festival team, and coached the 1991 gold-medal young rider team.

Kendra Carnes of Olympia, Washington, and Thriller during the Prix St. Georges test at the 1992 United States Dressage Federation's Region 6 Championships held at Donida Farm in Auburn, Washington. Owned by Don and Ida Morin, Donida Farm is one of the finest equestrian facilities in the Pacific Northwest.

ing that dressage is different from other equestrian disciplines. There's more of a partnership and a development of sensitivities between horse and rider in dressage. This takes many years to acquire, but the dressage rider has the time to cultivate that partnership because, on the average, dressage horses have longer careers than do horses in other disciplines."

No doubt another significant reason for the popularity of dressage is the ease with which a rider can begin training. All one needs are a horse, a saddle and an instructor. The novice dressage rider does not have to spend time constructing jumps or finding a large tract of open land on which to gallop or searching for water in which to go splashing. In fact, the beginner's saddle need not even be a dressage model. Any well-formed saddle will suffice as long as its shape encour-

After the ride comes the coach's review. Kendra Carnes, who has won both silver and bronze United States Dressage Federation medals, listens and learns following her Prix St. Georges test.

ages a rider to sit in its central and lowest part, thereby prompting a secure seat and correct posture.

Because dressage does not depend on special equipment or circumstances, says Robin Urmanic, rider liaison for the USDF, "people often come to dressage from another type of riding that requires particular provisions. For example, we get some western riders who may no longer have the resources to keep the cows on which to practice roping or cutting, but who are attracted by the idea of having a goal to work toward. They learn that there's no end to what you can do in dressage."

Dressage is also appealing because it does not pose the same risks to horse and rider as do some other equestrian disciplines, and seldom do riders go crashing to the ground in dressage. Thus, older riders can anticipate continued involvement with dressage—sometimes when their careers in other specialties are over—and younger riders (11 percent of all active USDF members are twenty-one or under) meet less resistance from their parents for wanting to participate in dressage than for wanting to enlist in some other mounted activities. Moreover, dressage wins many converts who discover that discipline is its own reward, who come to dressage with the notion that it is a means to an end, but who discover that it is an all-consuming end in its own right.

"And," says Baan, "the USET's bronze-medal win at the Olympics gave a boost to the sport that we're only now beginning to see." Indeed, if dressage grows as much in popularity during the next ten years as it did in the decade following the USET's last bronze-medal win in the Olympics, 1976, its future is golden.

According to the USDF, the reins of that future are in the hands of women. A 1990 USDF survey, which found that 84 percent of the organization's active riders are female, described the typical USDF participating member as "'thirtysomething,' a college graduate and a business executive or professional horsewoman" who spends "over twenty hours a week in a horse barn."

Dressage also attracts a wider base of noncompetitive riders, who "come in all sizes, shapes, and ages and from all walks of life," says Cathy Morelli, who has been teaching and competing in dressage for twenty-five years. "A lot of people who do dressage

While a friend reads out the required movements of the training-level dressage test, Lyn Brooks of Apopka, Florida, and Spellbound execute those movements. Clarcona Horseman's Park, which caters to a variety of equestrian activities, is operated by the Orange County Parks and Recreation Department.

Michael Poulin, a master of the classical art of dressage, uses a short-range radio headset to give instructions to the student he is watching carefully from ringside.

don't like to show. They just enjoy improving their horses' physiques and way of moving. They like the mental and physical challenge of dressage without the competitive side."

Although a novice can get started in dressage without special equipment, it takes a special horse both physically and mentally to compete seriously at the FEI (Fédération Equestre International) levels of dressage: Prix St. Georges, Intermediate I and II and Grand Prix.

Physically, "a dressage horse should have a good hind end, a strong topline with a sturdy, supple back, a neck that's set on fairly high out of the chest, good length and good angles in the hips, and correct legs," says Mary Alice Malone, whose Iron Spring Farm in southeastern Pennsylvania is a prominent breeding and training center.

"And when a horse moves," Malone continues, "it should be really active behind and, of course, loose and floating. Those attributes are nonnegotiable if you're trying to pick the ideal horse. You can negotiate on some of them if you don't have terribly high expectations, but the higher your expectations, the more your horse has to be correct because a horse is only as strong as its weakest link."

Strength is necessary in the hindquarters, particularly because FEI or upper-level dressage, for all its refinement and style, is strenuous on a horse. "At the upper levels you probably have more trouble behind with horses because they have to shift more weight back to their hindquarters," says Baan. "That requires tremendous muscular effort, and, therefore, dressage horses can have problems with soundness."

Even more important than strength and conformation is temperament, says Gray. "A horse must be willing to accept discipline from his rider, and he's got to have a certain concentration and willingness to work. You can overcome a lot of physical shortcomings if a horse will genuinely try for you, but no matter

Right
Michael Poulin and Graf George, riding down center line during the Grand Prix test at the 1993 Southern Comfort Dressage at Clarcona Horseman's Park, Orlando, Florida. Poulin and Graf George were members of the bronze medal–winning United States Equestrian Team's dressage team at the 1992 Olympics in Barcelona.

how much natural ability he might have, if he doesn't have the mind for dressage, you're beating your head against the wall."

Betsy Steiner, who rode on the USET's 1990 World Championship team, the 1991 bronze medal–winning Olympic sports festival team, and who coached the 1991 gold-medal young rider team, believes that "the warmblood is definitely the breed for dressage. But it's important to stress that any individual from any breed can become a very good dressage horse."

Among the warmbloods, Steiner prefers Dutch horses "because they're a little more sensitive, a little hotter in a good way, a little more keen and animated. I like that kind of horse better than one that's too methodical and not as quick to respond. But again, you will find some individuals with the former qualities in the other warmblood breeds—such as the German and Swedish warmbloods—too."

Most well-schooled English performance horses, no matter what their breeding, are capable of second-level dressage. At that point horses are expected to demonstrate a lengthened and a shortened stride at the walk, trot and canter, to perform small circles, to change leads through the walk, to do basic lateral work—leg yielding, shoulders-in, and haunches-in—and to master other elementary maneuvers. After second level, a distinction is made between horses that need dressage to help them in their primary activity and horses for whom dressage will be their primary activity. The latter, says Gray, will be asked "for real collection. They'll be asked to shift their weight back significantly and to sustain it. They'll be asked for more advanced lateral work, half-passes at trot and canter, and flying changes. At the fourth level you introduce canter pirouettes, and after that things start to come much more rapidly."

A horse's talent nurtured by a rider's skill and perserverance determines the amount of time a horse

Moments before their first-level test, Melody Miller and Tyranna warm up at the United States Dressage Federation's Region 6 Championships held at Donida Farm in Auburn, Washington.

As horse and rider progress through the various levels of competitive dressage, the movements they must perform become more demanding. The medium trot, which is introduced at second level tests, asks for more engagement from the horse than does the lengthening of stride required at first level. Maryanne Judkins of Wilsonville, Oregon, and Conversano II perform a medium trot at the United States Dressage Federation's Region 6 Championships held at Donida Farm, in Auburn, Washington.

Multiple exposures capture a succession of intricate movements performed by Tina Konyot of Stuart, Florida, and Ruben at the 1993 Southern Comfort Dressage at Clarcona Horseman's Park, Orlando, Florida.

spends at each competitive level. Not all dressage horses have the mental and physical attributes required at the FEI levels, and the rare horses that ascend all the way to Grand Prix competition usually take seven years or more to do so. But if Grand Prix horses are rare, so are Grand Prix riders.

"In many, many cases it's the rider, not the horse, that can't go on," says Gray. "A horse is not going to be any better than his rider can train him to be. There are a tremendous number of training and first-level horses, but even getting to second level catches up a lot of people. Then there's a pretty big jump to third level. The collection required there is what causes many people to hit a brick wall. I don't blame a lack of progress on the horse in most cases. I blame it on the rider."

Michael Poulin, a member of the USET's bronze-medal Olympic team, says that dressage riders, more than any others, need patience in order to succeed.

Fine engagement and elevation are displayed by Califa as he performs flying changes every third stride across the diagonal. Kamila duPont of West Palm Beach, Florida, guides Califa through this lilting maneuver during a Prix St. Georges test at the 1993 Southern Comfort Dressage held at Clarcona Horseman's Park.

Prego is well positioned to the right in a half-pass at a collected trot. Veteran rider Heidi Eriksen competes on Prego in a Grand Prix test at a 1988 Olympic selection trial held at the United States Equestrian Team headquarters in Gladstone, New Jersey. Eriksen, who has earned United States Dressage Federation gold, silver and bronze medals, is a certified American Horse Shows Association dressage judge.

Preparing to ride the corner of the arena at the canter in a first-level dressage test, fourteen-year-old Kathryn Poulin has Grey's Flag nicely bent at Clarcona Horseman's Park, Orlando, Florida. Kathryn is the daughter of Michael Poulin.

"This particular art does one major thing," says Poulin, "it develops people. They become more mature. Their judgment of a particular problem is geared by logic, not emotion. They become more focused on whether a horse is understanding what they're asking it to do, instead of simply trying to impose their will on the horse.

"A giver always succeeds more than a taker. The kinder the rider is, the more relaxed and pliable the horse becomes; and the more relaxed the horse is, the better it will go forward and do the things it is asked to do."

Even if competitive dressage were not the growing phenomenon it currently is, all riders would be in its debt because all horses, no matter what their employment, must be obedient, balanced and sensitive, must

Gillian Jones and Sophie's Choice achieve a beautiful extended trot in the first-level finals at the 1992 United States Dressage Federation's Region 6 Championships held at Donida Farm in Auburn, Washington.

move forward freely and willingly at any gait, and must be relaxed, submissive and attentive, responding calmly and promptly to their riders' aids.

Those virtues are instilled during gymnastic exercises in which riders employ subtle shifts of weight, leg pressure and light contact with the bit to produce horses that are bilaterally supple and that move in all gaits at an even tempo. Thus, the Quarter Horse with supernatural reactions cutting a calf from a herd, the grand prix jumper collecting itself to clear a huge oxer, the competitive trail horse picking its way meticulously up a steep hill, the polo pony zooming on a straight line toward the ball, the event horse instinctively adjusting its stride as it negotiates the elements of a bank, all perform better for having been schooled in dressage.

The popularity of dressage has not been confined to the training ring and the show ring. Spectators in significant numbers have discovered dressage, too. This discovery is somewhat remarkable because the scoring system in dressage is thoroughly subjective. Although letters placed around the dressage arena—which is either a 20 x 40- or 20 x 60-meter rectangle—inform the riders where to begin and where to conclude the movements required in a test, spectators cannot tell whether a dressage horse is performing with sufficient impulsion as easily as they can tell whether a show jumper has cleared a fence without knocking any rails down.

A dressage rider is evaluated according to a written standard and receives a score that ranges from 0 to 10 for each movement in a test. The scores for a few of the most important movements in a test are counted double. Zero is awarded if a movement is not executed. A score of 10 means that the movement was performed without flaw. At the end of a test, the scores earned by a rider are tallied, and points earned are divided by the total points possible, which yields a percentage score.

Unlike human gymnastics, where 10s are not altogether unusual and an average score of 9-plus is the norm, dressage scores are rather lower. For example, the individual gold medalist at the 1992 Olympics

These spectators have a three-ring seat at the 1992 Summer Dressage Fest in Grass Lake, Michigan. The Summer Fest has been held at the Waterloo Hunt Club in rural Grass Lake, twenty-five miles from Ann Arbor, Michigan, for more than fifteen years.

Sharon Lewis of Wheaton, Illinois, and Wred Wrum execute an extended trot across the diagonal during a fourth-level test at the 1992 Summer Dressage Fest in Grass Lake, Michigan. Lewis is a United States Dressage Federation advanced junior young rider. This classification is given to riders under twenty-one who are competing at fourth level and above. She is also a USDF bronze-medal rider, which means that she has earned scores of at least 60 percent in four first, second, or third level events.

Left
The best seat in the house belongs to Kelly Boyle of Oak Harbor, Washington. Before riding in the first-level junior championship dressage test at the 1992 United States Dressage Federation's Region 6 Championships held at Donida Farm in Auburn, Washington, Boyle watches other riders in the class from her vantage point on Zeki Ben Mar. Boyle's mother, Marie, has a video camera ready to record the ride.

scored 79.31 percent, which is just about the numerical equivalent of a "good" rating according to the FEI. In the FEI grading system, a score of 6 is deemed satisfactory, 7 is fairly good, 8 is good, 9 is very good and 10 is excellent.

The scoring system in dressage is like that of a notoriously tough-grading professor. "You don't see 90 percent rides in dressage," says Baan. "And you never see 100 percent rides. A score around 80 percent is a rare exception.

"Actually, the adjectives are probably one grade below where they should be. I think an 80 percent dressage ride would be *verrrry* good. A 7 is called fairly good, but a 70 percent ride is really a good ride."

For the dedicated student, the attention to detail, not the scoreboard, is important. Dressage, in the purest sense of the word, is a self-centered activity.

"My excitement comes from riding a perfect twenty-meter circle," says Gray. "It's difficult to convey to a nondressage rider the phenomenal challenge of riding a twenty-meter circle correctly. To many people that's boring, but I can take a horse out and spend an hour perfecting a circle just for the challenge of making myself and my horse the best we can be."

Carol Lavell of Fairfax, Vermont, and Gifted during the Grand Prix Special at the 1991 Festival of Champions held at the United States Equestrian Team headquarters in Gladstone. After winning nine horse of the year and national championships in six years, Gifted was the Miller/USET's national Grand Prix champion, the United States Dressage Federation Grand Prix Horse of the Year, and the winner of the FEI Volvo World Cup U.S. League Final in 1991. In 1992 he and Lavell were members of the bronze medal–winning USET Olympic dressage team. They won the FEI Volvo World Cup U.S. League Final for the second year in a row in 1992, and Gifted was once again the Miller/USET's National Grand Prix Champion.

Jane Savoie of Randolph Center, Vermont, rides Zapatero at an extended trot during the United States Equestrian Team's Grand Prix championship at the 1991 Festival of Champions held at USET headquarters in Gladstone, New Jersey. Savoie is a United States Dressage Federation gold, silver and bronze medalist.

Left
Approaching the corner of the ring, Lisa Schreifels of Burlington, Washington, indicates by the position of her left hand that she is preparing Macintosh for a turn to the left during a working trot at the United States Dressage Federation's Region 6 Championships held at Donida Farm, in Auburn, Washington.

Before riding her training-level test at the 1993 Southern Comfort Dressage competition at Clarcona Horseman's Park, Orlando, Florida, Nancy Dau longes Weiss Gold in a warmup ring. Dau is a United States Dressage Federation qualified rider, which means that she has earned four scores of 60 percent or higher in training level competition.

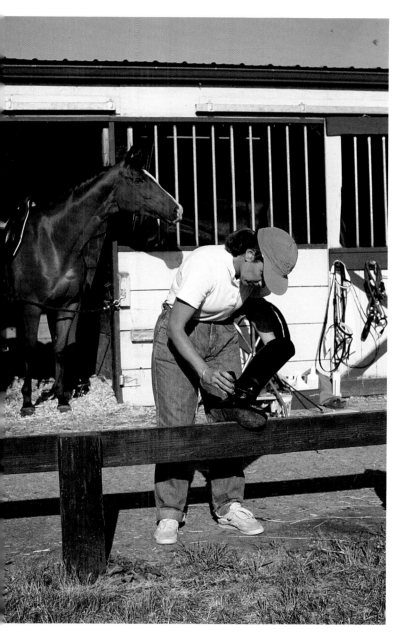

Before putting her best foot forward in a first-level test, Theresa Cotterell of Longview, Washington, polishes her boots.

The mark of a successful rider. Rosettes for first-, fifth- and third-place finishes hang cheek by jowl with snaffle bridle, halter, lead shank and red garment bag.

Kathy Von Ertfelda of South Dartmouth, Massachusetts, riding Dondolo in the Grand Prix test at the 1993 Southern Comfort Dressage held at Clarcona Horseman's Park, Orlando, Florida. Von Ertfelda is a United States Dressage Federation gold-medal rider. To earn this designation a rider must receive scores of 60 percent or higher in at least two intermediate-level rides and two grand prix–level rides.

Left

An international competitor for more than thirty years, Jessica Ransehausen of Unionville, Pennsylvania, has won a United States Dressage Federation gold medal, has competed in the 1987 World Cup Finals in Hanover, Germany, and has placed third in the Grand Prix at Zuidlaren, Holland. In addition, Ransehausen, a dressage judge, was the chef d'equipe for the United States Equestrian Team's bronze medal–winning dressage team in 1992. Here Ransehausen canters into a corner on the Dutch Warmblood Orpheus at the 1988 Olympic selection trials held at USET headquarters in Gladstone, New Jersey.

After reining back four steps at A, Charlotte Bayley and Chardonnay proceed at a collected walk during a fourth-level test at the 1992 Summer Dressage Fest in Grass Lake, Michigan. Bayley, who lives in Newbury, Ohio, is a dressage instructor as well as a competitor.

Kathy Beyer of Rockledge, Florida, and Eliten executing the collected walk on the long side of the arena during their Prix St. Georges test at the 1993 Southern Comfort Dressage at Clarcona Horseman's Park, Orlando, Florida. The Prix St. Georges is the first of the upper, or FEI (Fédération Equestre International), levels of dressage. The others are Intermediate I and II and Grand Prix.

Dr. Jorge Gomez and 16.1-hand, thirteen-year-old Andalusian stallion Pregonero performing an 8-meter circle at A during a fourth-level test at the 1992 Summer Dressage Fest in Grass Lake, Michigan.

Debra Wiedmaier-Dutta of North Tarrytown, New York, and Jasmine De Bray A compete in the
$3,500 FEI Intermediate II class at the 1991 Central Florida Dressage Classic. This competition is
held at the Palm Beach Polo and Equestrian Club. Wiedmaier-Dutta is a United States Dressage Federation gold, silver and bronze medalist.

Cantering down center line after completing a left half-pass
during an Open Prix St. Georges test, Alicia Salazar of
Dundee, Illinois, and Rushonne are ready to track left at the
1991 Festival of Champions held at the United States
Equestrian Team's headquarters, in Gladstone, New Jersey.
This young rider also competed in the M & M's Chocolate
Candies young rider selection classes. This annual series
seeks to identify promising young dressage riders throughout the United States.

Five-time national freestyle champion Robert Dover looks pleased with Federleicht's performance as they　salute the judges at the 1988 Olympic selection trials held at the United States Equestrian Team's headquarters in Gladstone, New Jersey. First long listed by the USET in 1977 when he was twenty-one, Dover made his international debut as a member of the 1984 USET Olympic team on Romantico. They were also members of the gold medal–winning teams at the 1985 and 1989 North American Dressage Championship. Dover came out of retirement to help the USET's Olympic dressage team win a bronze medal in Barcelona in 1992.

Wachmann gets a pat on the neck as he and Cathy Morelli of Bedminster, New Jersey, leave the ring at a free walk following the Open Prix St. Georges test at the 1991 Festival of Champions held at the United States Equestrian Team headquarters in Gladstone, New Jersey. Morelli, a United States Dressage Federation gold-medal rider, has been teaching and competing in dressage for twenty-five years. She won the FEI Volvo World Cup League in the U.S. in 1990.

EVENTING

Eventing has been called the ultimate equestrian challenge, and not without reason. The event horse is the embodiment of courage, speed, dexterity, power, scope, precision, durability and a resolute will to prevail. The event rider, while possessing similar virtues in plentiful measure, must be able to elicit from a horse, within prudent limits, the willingness to deliver its talents on request, no matter how challenging the obstacle or how taxing the pace.

The three-day (or combined training) event was designed originally to measure the fortitude of military horses and their inclination to soldier on in service to their riders. Although there is no longer a practical need for the kind of equine valor the three-day event was designed to identify, the celebration of that valor remains the incentive for a growing legion of three-day competitors throughout the world.

On Day 1 of a three-day event, a rider must bend a ready-to-run, burstingly fit horse to the meticulous, prescribed movements of a dressage test, which is sim-ilar to driving a race-tuned Maserati smoothly at slow speeds in second gear without riding the clutch. On Day 2, known as speed-and-endurance day, horse and rider confront a four-part adventure that begins with an exercise called roads-and-tracks, in which they must cover several thousand meters at a designated pace. After finishing roads-and-tracks, they must jump a steeplechase course within a specified time limit, then set off immediately on roads-and-tracks once more, again covering several thousand meters at a designated pace. Following a brief intermission for a veterinary inspection, horse and rider must conquer a one- to four-and-a-half-mile cross-country course on which are set fifteen to thirty-five formidable obstacles. The total distance traveled during speed and endurance can range from just under twelve to almost nineteen miles. The length of the cross-country course, the number and size of the obstacles encountered there, and the time allotted to complete the course vary with the competitive level of the event. On Day 3 a show jumping course, created to verify a horse's

Left
Determined not to let this coffin jump lay to rest her chances, Terri Buzan from West Chicago, Illinois, pushes Five Star General forward in the open intermediate division of the 1991 Essex Three-Day Event, at Gladstone, New Jersey. Buzan, who usually competes and holds down a full-time job, finished second in the Trojan-Horse Ranch Horse Trials, intermediate division, in 1992 and fourth in the Centel-Wayne Dupage Horse Trials, advanced division, that same year.

An event horse is nothing if not versatile, jumping a steeplechase fence in a flat trajectory and jumping a cross-country fence with greater scope. The flatter, faster jumping style is neces- sary on a steeplechase course because the required speed is faster than that required on cross country. Sharon Sterzer of Richardsville, Virginia, and Peeping Tom scamper through the steeplechase course in the senior preliminary division at the 1989 Essex Three-Day Event at Gladstone, New Jersey.

ability and inclination to continue in service, awaits all competitors that have met the first days' requirements. Not surprisingly, the number of horses finishing any event is always smaller than the number of horses that started it.

Event riders must be jacks (and jills) of all equestrian trades and masters of one: the cross-country course. "That's the real meat of our sport," says event rider Mimi Bertolet of West Grove, Pennsylvania. "I just love to run and jump."

According to one former president of the United States Combined Training Association USCTA), the ability to run and jump on a cross-country course is "what sets both the event horse and the event rider apart from—perhaps even beyond—most others. It's the phase a competitor remembers best about horse trials. It's what gains a reputation for an event. It's what the rider most wants to know about as he trains and schools his horse."

Indeed, there is better, more refined, more elegant

The Kentucky landscape appears to be moving in fast forward as Lellie Ward and Paddle go wooshing by at the 1987 Rolex Kentucky advanced selection trials for the Pan-American Games. In order to complete the 6,555-meter (4.07-mile) course without incurring any time penalties, riders must maintain an average speed of 570 meters per minute. (That's 21 miles an hour for those of you still committed to the English measuring system.)

dressage to be seen elsewhere. There are far more technical and difficult fences to be negotiated in open jumper classes on the grand prix circuit. There are more demanding steeplechase courses at hunt meets. But nowhere are there challenges that require more skill, courage and tenacity than does the cross-country course, where horses that have put in what would constitute a full day's work for the average horse are required to press on at a persistent gallop, jumping onto and off steep banks, leaping into and out of water and hurling themselves over one massive, unforgiving wooden barrier after another. It is a task not without risk, a position for which the faint of heart, the unprepared and the uninspired need not apply.

But, says Bertolet, "we train for those risks every day. We prepare for them through dressage training and cross-country schooling; through foxhunting, which teaches a horse to gallop boldly and carefully; and through schooling our horses in show jumping classes at hunter shows."

For its part the USCTA attempts to prepare horse and rider for the challenges they will face on course by meting out those challenges in escalating increments of difficulty over five competitive levels: novice, training, preliminary, intermediate and advanced. Thus, cross-country fences are never more than 2'11" high at the novice level, no fence at that level has a spread more than a few inches beyond 4 feet, and the distances between the elements of an obstacle do not require unusual striding. At the advanced level, however, fences

Steeds passing in the light, one near the start, the other near the finish of the Essex Three-Day Event, which is held annually at Hamilton Farm in Gladstone, New Jersey, headquarters of the United States Equestrian Team. Nearly thirty years old, Essex is one of three two-star competitions in North America. Only three three-star events on this continent—Rolex in Kentucky, Fair Hill in Maryland, and Checkmate in Ontario, Canada—rank higher.

are as much as a foot higher than at the novice level, most spreads are one or two feet wider and multiple obstacles may require shortening or lengthening of stride as well as acceleration or deceleration in the approach to a fence.

Most riders with a reasonably fit horse and a reasonable amount of time and talent are capable of competing at some level of combined training. For three out of four riders, that level is either novice or training, where horse trials and combined tests, both of which are abbreviated versions of three-day events, are the sole competitions offered.

A horse trial, which can take place over one, two or three days, does not require the roads-and-tracks or steeplechase phases of speed-and-endurance. A com-

bined test comprises dressage and show jumping only and is always held in one day.

Horse trials and combined tests may be offered at all competitive levels—novice through advanced—but full-scale three-day events are held only at preliminary, intermediate and advanced levels. (Some three-day events are compressed into two days. Dressage and show jumping are held the first day, and a complete speed-and-endurance phase is held the second day.)

In order to qualify for their first three-day event, both horse and rider must have completed four preliminary-level horse trials—either separately or as a team. Moreover, both must have made their way around two of those horse trials without any jumping penalties on cross country.

Left
Jiffy Read of Winchester, Massachusetts, and Lotus, a 17-hand Dutch Warmblood, on course in the open intermediate division at the 1989 Essex Three-Day Event, Gladstone, New Jersey. Read and Lotus were winners of advanced horse trials at Fair Hill, Maryland, in 1990 and 1992 and of an open intermediate horse trial at the Walthour-Moss Foundation in 1991.

CCI one star division-rider Ashley MacVaugh appears to be standing on the brakes while the hard-charging Midnight Rover heads into the Mercky Water jump at the 1990 Radnor Hunt International Three-Day Event. This event, first organized in 1974, benefits the Paoli Memorial Hospital and the Radnor Hunt Pony Club.

The preliminary level is where the training wheels come off for combined-training riders. "At the novice and training levels you're really introducing building blocks," says course designer Roger Haller, who fashioned the world championship course at Lexington, Kentucky, in 1978. "You're saying, 'Jump the vertical, jump the oxer, jump the sloping spread. Jump the ditch, jump the brush, get your feet wet. Jump onto a bank, jump down a drop.' There is an interesting progression that begins at the training level, though, because training is where you start to see cross-country riding as opposed to people going out and jumping one fence after another."

By training level the maximum height of fences is 3'3", ditches begin to appear on cross-country courses and there must be one jumping effort either into or out of water. There is a considerable reduction in the number of starters between novice and training levels.

Nearly half of all combined-training starters, 46 percent, compete on the novice level, but only 30 percent compete in training-level events.

As courses become more difficult at the intermediate and advanced levels of eventing, course designers seek to "stretch the imagination and challenge the ability of the rider," says Haller. At the same time, they must continue to design courses that fit neatly into the available landscape.

"Course design involves planning out the best track for your site, a natural track that has to work first for the horses and then for the people watching the event. You also have to spread out the difficult fences and decide how you want to lead the horses and riders to those fences, how you will back off and provide breathing spaces between them and how you will ease up at the end. Laying out the track and distributing the problem fences are unique to each event

Lisa Anderson and Volterra are about to be sent out by the starter onto the preliminary-level cross-country course at the 1992 Centel Wayne-Dupage Horse Trials. The starter is one of hundreds of volunteers, who have been called the unsung heroes and heroines of eventing. Their work must be done so the show can go on.

site. You can't simply decide the kinds of fences you want before you've even looked at a piece of property and put those fences up, regardless of whether they fit the contours of the land. That approach might give you a collection of nice fences—if you have a good course builder—but it won't give you a good course. This is one of the reasons why some courses ride well and others do not."

Horses that can carry riders successfully through novice- and training-level horse trials, can also, in some cases, make the step up to preliminary events. But the small number of riders, roughly 5 percent of all starters, at the intermediate and advanced levels find fewer and fewer horses capable of competing at those levels, especially in advanced three-day events. The physical and mental skills required of an advanced-level horse are well beyond the ordinary horse's gifts, and the toll exacted by the years of training required to reach the advanced level—most horses spend at least one year at each competitive plateau—are well beyond the ordinary horse's tolerance. Only the strongest survive, and even they are not asked to do more than two three-day events a year once they reach the advanced level, one in the spring and one in the fall with two or three horse trials by way of preparation.

Event horses on their way up through the ranks have a more active schedule. A horse slated to compete in a preliminary three-day event at the end of June, for example, will have put in thirty days of walking work and thirty days of dressage and flat work before beginning serious training around April 1. That horse might compete in as many as five horse trials at two- or three-week intervals in the twelve weeks before the three-day event. On the days in be-

The saddle and the pickup truck are well polished, but the mud on the truck tire suggests there might be deep going at the Fair Hill Spring Horse Trials in Fair Hill, Maryland.

tween those competitions a horse may go for a one-and-a-half-hour walk or a one-hour walk followed by either thirty or forty-five minutes of dressage or a couple of turns around a show jumping course. Other days will be devoted to the equine version of wind sprints: perhaps three five-minute trots at 220 meters per minute (mpm) with two-minute rests in between followed by three six-minute gallops at 400 mpm with two-minute rests in between.

Left
David O'Connor and Wilton Fair jumping the first element of a coffin obstacle at the 1990 Fair Hill Spring Horse Trials in Fair Hill, Maryland. This team won the 1990 Rolex Kentucky advanced Three-Day Event. Had Wilton Fair, who earned the highest scores in the selection trials for the 1992 Olympics, not gone lame a week before the games, he and O'Connor would have represented the United States in Barcelona.

Overleaf
Karen Lende and Nos Ecus gallop between jumps on the advanced division cross-country course at the 1990 Fair Hill Spring Horse Trials in Maryland. As a ten-year-old in 1989, this 16.1-hand, Anglo-Arab bay gelding, foaled in France, won the United States Equestrian Team's fall three-day event championship. The following year he was third at the Rolex Kentucky Three-Day Event and was on the short list for the world championships in Stockholm. In 1991 he won the advanced horse trials at Fair Hill in Maryland and at Tetbury in the United Kingdom.

Local favorite Kelly Joesten from Rockford, Illinois, sails over a cross-country fence on Sansibar in the advanced division at the 1992 Centel Wayne-Dupage Horse Trials. This is the only advanced division horse trials in the Midwest, and it is one of fewer than fifteen such events held in the United States annually.

Most of the horses that reach the advanced level are Thoroughbreds, either full or in large part. "I prefer them for eventing," says Deanna Hines. A young West Coast rider who has competed on two breeds, Hines won a preliminary three-day on a warmblood and an intermediate event on a Thoroughbred at the same competition while still in her teens.

"My thoroughbred was not a good mover, but he was a good runner," says Hines. "My warmblood was a good mover, but he didn't have the ability to go really fast. That limited him for upper-level eventing."

No matter what the breed, an event horse must have certain qualities. "The first thing I look for is a big eye with a tremendous amount of honesty and expression," says Torrance Watkins, a team gold medalist at the 1984 Olympics. "That expression is called 'the look of eagles.' Some horses may not have it and might still end up being great, but it's something you look for nevertheless.

"In conformation I look for good feet, short bones, short cannons (to take the stress off the tendons), a nice sloping shoulder, a good angle from hip to hock, a good angle from hip to second thigh and hock, powerful quarters and a neck well placed on the shoulder. We put so much stress on event horses that it's nice to start with the most ideal conformation you can find. But that doesn't mean the odd horse won't come along, one that lacks some of those characteristics but is still successful."

Right
Michlynn Sterling and her Connemara pony, Balius Kerry Blue, leaping a quartet of horizontal telephone poles on the open intermediate division cross-country course at the 1993 Trojan-Horse Ranch Horse Trials, Cave Creek, Arizona. The two weekends of eventing at Cave Creek at the end of February and the beginning of March are part of the West of the Rockies Circuit, which also features competitions at Ram Tap and Wild Horse Valley Ranch in California.

Allison Greerlee of Boulder, Colorado, and Valley Girl pass two of the distinctive white cupolas on the barns at the Lamplight Equestrian Center during the dressage phase of the 1992 Centel Wayne-Dupage Horse Trials. The Lamplight center in Wayne, Illinois, thirty-four miles west of Chicago, is one of the Midwest's top equestrian facilities. The Wayne-Dupage Horse Trials, held annually at the Lamplight center, were voted best event of 1991 by the United States Combined Training Association.

Through competition and conditioning, the event rider is taking the measure of his or her horse. That knowledge is crucial, says Bruce Davidson, individual world champion in 1974 and 1978 and team gold medalist at the 1976 and 1984 Olympics. "The successful cross-country rider must know all of a horse's attributes and shortcomings in order to anticipate a situation and compensate for it before it becomes a problem."

Above all, adds Denny Emerson, a former Olympic Team member and two-term past president of the USCTA, the successful rider is a good horseman. "That has got to be the underlying principle of combined training," says Emerson. "Good horsemen do not create situations that abuse horses. People involved in eventing should think of everything they do in terms of good horsemanship: the course designer who builds a course, the technical delegate who checks it, the ground jury that oversees it, the rider on the course, and the coach who's telling the rider what to do. A good horseman isn't someone who wins gold medals, it's somebody who puts the welfare of the horse first."

Successful eventers cannot neglect their own fitness in preparing for an event either. Their training, like that of their horses', requires ongoing effort. "I

Left
Fresca, a seventeen-year-old pony, carries Pali Pearson, five years her junior, of Puyallup, Washington, across a water obstacle in the junior novice division at the Mountain Meadows Horse Trials, North Bend, Washington. Junior novice competition, which is offered at the event committee's discretion, is an entry-level class meant to give riders a taste of eventing and chance to decide if that taste is to their liking.

Jim Graham and Easter Parade take the corner option at this fence at the 1992 Centel Wayne-Dupage Horse Trials. Graham, who lives in Florence, Alabama, was the eventual winner of this advanced event. He and Easter Parade won ten three-day events and horse trials from the open preliminary to the advanced level between 1989 and 1992, including four in a row between February and April 1989.

ride a lot of horses every day and I lift weights," says Jil Walton, the highest-finishing American rider at the 1992 Olympics. "I work out on a regular basis with a personal trainer.

"And because so much of this sport is mental, I try to stay in a positive attitude by making sure that all the little details have been taken care of—that I've done my homework with my horse, I'm fit, and I'm not worried about anything else."

The love of running and jumping does not appear to have gone unrequited among event riders during the last decade. Between 1980 and 1990 the number of starters in USCTA-sanctioned events increased by

65 percent, from 15,394 in 1980 to 25,409 in 1990. During the same time the numbers of spectators at three-day events increased accordingly. The Rolex Kentucky Three-Day Event, the best known in the United States, draws 50,000 spectators annually. Large crowds also attend the other three-star, advanced-level events in North America—Fair Hill in Maryland and Checkmate near Toronto, Canada—as well as two-star competitions at Gladstone, New Jersey; Radnor, Pennsylvania; and Bromont, in Quebec province, near Montreal, Canada.

(There are two regularly scheduled four-star three-day events in the world: Burghley and Badminton in

Right
With a cloud of dust and a hearty, Hi-ho-Silver leap, Dorothy Trapp from Lexington, Kentucky, and Adonis momentarily defy gravity at a rails-and-drop fence on the senior preliminary cross-country course at the 1988 Essex Three-Day Event in Gladstone, New Jersey.

Noel Parker-Ortiz of Twain Harte, California, and Irish Luck clear the Oxer Massif on the advanced cross-country course at the Trojan-Horse Ranch Horse Trials, Cave Creek, Arizona. Parker-Ortiz's other mount in this competition, Tell the Shrink, was the winner of this event and of the Wild Horse Valley Ranch advanced horse trial in 1992.

England. The quadrennial Olympic three-day event is also four stars, as are the quadrennial world championships, held during even-numbered years between Olympics.)

Event promoters, like their counterparts at hunter-jumper shows, provide more than the main event by way of entertainment at a three-day. "We're an extravaganza as well as a competition," says Jane Atkinson, director of the Rolex Kentucky Three-Day Event. "We

have the trade fair. We have exhibitions. And we have other activities. But not too many. We don't want to detract from people watching the competition because eventing is such a dynamic sport to watch."

Indeed, it is the excitement that horses generate that brings people to equestrian events. Because of this excitement, because of the magnificent sport horses and the people dedicated to them, our glorious equestrian traditions live on.

Dyana Lynd-Pugh and Escalon leapfrog the Jack Le Goff Amusement Park fence on the open preliminary cross-country course at the 1993 Trojan-Horse Ranch Horse Trials. One of the few cross-country fences named after a person, the Jack Le Goff honors the man who coached the USET three-day event team from 1970 through 1984, a period in which the United States won gold medals at the 1974 World Championships, the 1975 Pan-American Games and the 1976 and 1984 Olympics.

This space for hire. A creative example of putting on the dog at the 1993 Trojan-Horse Ranch Horse Trials, Cave Creek, Arizona.

Competitors often are the most interested spectators at three-day events. Michael Godfrey of Oldwick, New Jersey, watches a fellow rider leave the start box on cross-country day at the Fair Hill International Three-Day Event, held each fall in Fair Hill, Maryland.

Right
Karen Lende of Upperville, Virginia, and Park Hall send the water flying upward at the Chesapeake Water and Dock obstacle during the fall 1990 Fair Hill International Three-Day Event, advanced division. Lende, who married fellow eventer David O'Connor in 1993, is best known for her success with The Optimist, who was retired at the 1991 Rolex Kentucky Three-Day Event and Horse Trials, where Lende won the advanced division on Mr. Maxwell.

Jil Walton and her ex-racehorse Patrona at the drop jump on the advanced-division cross-country course at the 1993 Trojan-Horse Ranch Horse Trials, Cave Creek, Arizona. Walton and Patrona were the highest-finishing U.S. pair at the 1992 Olympics in Barcelona, a remarkable accomplishment for a rider who had been competing at the advanced level for only a year before the Olympics and a horse that was seven years old, the minimum Olympic age.

Right
While judges watch from a horse trailer cleverly disguised as a judging stand, Torrance Watkins and Argyle Chief navigate the dressage test at the Radnor International Three-Day Event. Watkins leaped onto the eventing stage in the mid-1970s when she took a four-year-old Appaloosa called Bonanza's Little Dandy from the novice to the advanced level in two years. She is best known, however, for her partnership with a smallish, 15.1-hand pinto mare named Poltroon. The irrepressible, crowd-pleasing pair was a startling second at Burghley, England, in 1979, and Watkins was the United States Combined Training Association's leading lady rider that year and several years thereafter.

Leaving a small cloud of dust behind, Ralph Hill of Wayne, Illinois, and the Polish Trakehner gelding Neron make the Jenny Lane crossing, the twentieth of twenty-five obstacles in the advanced division at the 1987 Rolex Kentucky Three-Day Event and Horse Trials. Hill and Neron placed third in this selection trial for the 1987 Pan-American Games.

Some cross-country fences are designed to give a horse and rider the confidence needed for bigger challenges over the next hill. This open intermediate fence, the Turning Logs, at the 1992 Mountain Meadows Horse Trials at North Bend, Washington, is one such confidence builder for Dorothy Hamilton and Flyer. The course at Mountain Meadows was designed by Todd Trewin, a member of the USET's 1992 Olympic three-day team.

Anna Collier of Dever Island, Oregon, and Rots of Ruck taking it to the Jackson Bank at the 1992 Mountain Meadows Horse Trials in North Bend, Washington. Collier and Rots of Ruck both appear to be looking for a safe landing on the other side of this open intermediate bank.

Jennifer Franks and The Kid's Krazy splashing through the water element of Henley's Hollow on the open preliminary cross-country course at the 1993 Trojan-Horse Ranch Trials, Cave Creek, Arizona. Because horses do not take to water naturally, some schooling is needed to prepare them for the water obstacles they will meet at events.

Lisa Johansson of Quebec, and Khatmandu are about to get
their feet wet at the Head of the Lake, a Normandy bank
on the advanced-division cross-country course, at the 1991
Rolex Kentucky Three-Day Event. This fence offers horse
and rider 3'10" slanted rails, a 4'11" spread, and 3'4"
slanted rails with a six-foot drop into the water. Tradition-
ally one of the most difficult fences on the Lexington cross-
country course, the Head of the Lake asks riders to choose
between bouncing off the Normandy bank into the lake or
trying to make their horses put in a short stride before
jumping into the water. Khatmandu negotiated this fence
but was retired the next day during show jumping.

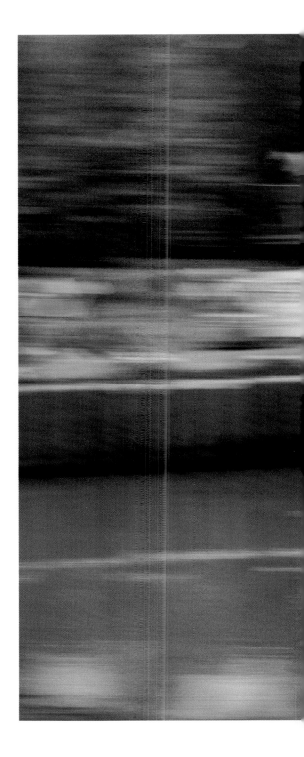

Wash Bishop of Middleburg, Virginia, surfing through a water obstacle on the Thoroughbred-Hanoverian cross Furst Falco at the 1991 Rolex Kentucky open intermediate horse trials. A capable, veteran rider, Bishop finished second in this division at Lexington. Later in the year he won a preliminary division on Anglo-Saxon at the Radnor Hunt International Three-Day Event in Radnor, Pennsylvania.

A full house at the 1992 Rolex Kentucky Three-Day Event watches two-time world champion Bruce Davidson as he pilots Happy Talk through the first day's dressage test. Like jockeys who secure a good position out of the starting gate, eventers with the best scores in dressage are sitting pretty for the next two days' activities. Thus, Happy Talk, who was second after dressage, still finished a creditable eighth for the entire event, despite incurring penalties on cross-country and in show jumping.

Jane Sleeper of Warwick, Maryland, and the Irish-bred gelding Carpe Diem during the show jumping phase of the 1991 Essex Three-Day Event, open intermediate division. Sleeper and Carpe Diem placed seventh in this event. According to the United States Combined Training Association, the "sole object" of show jumping "is to prove that on the day after speed-and-endurance horses have retained the suppleness, energy, and obedience necessary for them to continue."

"I ride an old Paint . . ." Or pinto to you tenderfeet. Fancy Lad, ridden by Mary Knievel, Evel's daughter-in-law, does an extended walk through a landscape that looks as though it were borrowed from a Clint Eastwood western. The actual setting is the dressage test, senior training level, at the 1993 Trojan-Horse Ranch Horse Trials, Cave Creek, Arizona.

Canadian rider Jamie Smart and Glendevlin, a ten-year-old, 16.3-hand Thoroughbred, in flight at the 1991 Rolex Kentucky Three-Day Event. The twenty-second of twenty-seven imposing obstacles on the cross-country course in Lexington, this 3'7" Trakehner is located at the bottom of a bank and is perched above a six-foot-wide ditch that resembles an open grave. Smart, who finished tenth on Glendevlin and ninth on Cornerstone, was the only rider to place on two horses in this division.

The Giant's Table on the advanced division cross-country course at the 1988 Rolex Mid-Florida Pony Club Spring Horse Trials elicits a giant effort from Ireland's Kim Baker and Morning Glow. In addition to being an international event, the RM-FPCSHT, held in Altoona, Florida, was one of several selection trials for riders hoping to represent the United States at the Seoul Olympics.

Horses are examined for soundness several times during a three-day event. On a Saturday at Radnor in 1990, a young groom jogs a horse for the veterinarian's inspection.

Left
While waiting to go out onto the cross-country course at the 1990 Radnor International Three-Day Event, Torrance Watkins, who once had a career in high-fashion cosmetics, watches as David Taylor applies lubricating cream to Argylle Chief's legs. The cream helps a horse to slide across, instead of getting hung up on, any fence he might encounter too closely.

Like a race car in the pit at Indianapolis, Nos Ecus stands motionless while rider Karen Lende O'Connor (left, mid-ground) and a crew of grooms and attendants get him ready for the cross-country phase of the Essex Three-Day Event in Gladstone, New Jersey. After completing the first three phases of speed-and-endurance, horses are examined by veterinarians and attended by rider and pit crews in the ten-minute box before going out on the cross-country course.

The elephant-trap fence, deployed by course designer Roger Haller at the Essex Three-Day Event in Gladstone, New Jersey, is a fixture on many cross-country courses. Open intermediate competitor Rick Wallace and Ultimate Trial get over this one handily.

Bat in hand, flak jacket, high-tech watches, riding cap, and shadow goggles in place, Abigail Lufkin stands in the ten-minute box before tackling the junior preliminary cross-country course at the 1991 Essex Three-Day Event at Gladstone, New Jersey.

Doubling as a valet, a mountain bike holds a competitor's helmet, back protector and bridle.

This ecologically correct barrier, fashioned out of wine barrels from local wineries, was the last obstacle on the senior training-level cross-country course at the 1992 Mountain Meadows Horse Trials, North Bend, Washington. Denise Konetchy of Troy, Idaho, and Bo Rock Ka Loo pop over the barrels easily.

*Left
Mount Si on the western flank of the Cascade Mountain Range shrinks Carrie Huffman and Lurena down to movieland size. Huffman was competing here in the senior novice division at the 1992 Mountain Meadows Horse Trials in North Bend, Washington.*

Stuart Young-Black and Von Perrier having an easy time of it at the Log-on-a-Lump jump at the 1991 Rolex Kentucky Three-Day Event. The Canadian rider from Orangeville, Ontario, went on to win this advanced, three-star event, one of only three of its kind in North America. In 1991 Young-Black also was a member of the Canadian gold medal–winning team at the Pan-American Championships in north Georgia.

All decked out in red and blue, and riding the near-white Shakedown Street, Mimi Bertolet of West Grove, Pennsylvania, vies for a place on the United States Equestrian Team's three-day event squad at the Rolex Kentucky Three-Day in 1992. The best-attended, most prestigious three-day in North America, Kentucky was also the final U.S. selection trial for the Barcelona Olympics. More than 50,000 people attend this event in Lexington each year, gathering around the cross-country jumps like the gallery assembles around each hole at the Masters Golf tournament in Augusta, Georgia.

Excellent cuisine and dazzling fall colors are trademarks of the Radnor International Three-Day Event. For Janice Binkley and The Rogue, however, the foliage is a distant backdrop as they school before the dressage test at their first three-day competition. In order to qualify for a three-day event, horse and rider must complete several preliminary-level horse trials.

Many cross-country jumps offer riders one or more options for getting over them. The most direct, and most difficult, routes are generally the quickest. Matthew Firestone of Waterford, Virginia, takes Santex over the first element of The Spider, a four-part fence in the advanced division at the 1987 Rolex Kentucky Three-Day Event.

Michael Godfrey, eventual winner in the senior preliminary division of the 1988 Essex Three-Day Event in Gladstone, New Jersey, steers Duffy Moon through a water obstacle on the cross-country course. In 1990 Godfrey campaigned Shannon, a 16.2-hand bay mare who was then ten, to the United States Combined Training Association's Horse of the Year honors. Shannon, who is owned by Jacqueline Vogel, is now ridden by Karen Lende O'Connor.

In three-day eventing horse and rider must attack a course with courage and determination. Only two fences from the finish line, Karin Balling is well out of the saddle as Warlock bursts out of the water with no lack of determination at the 1992 Centel Wayne-Dupage Horse Trials, intermediate division.

Right
While Allean Wardle looks ahead, Chort looks down carefully before dropping off a bank on the cross-country course at the Trojan-Horse Ranch Horse Trials, Cave Creek, Arizona. This bank was the third of seventeen obstacles on the open preliminary course. At the advanced level, two steps above preliminary, courses may have twice as many obstacles.

The obstacles on a cross-country course resemble the illustrations from a children's book about giants. The Table jump at the 1992 Centel Wayne-Dupage Horse Trials is no exception. Katie Cauwenberg and Crescende display their table manners on the intermediate course.

Charge Commander takes command of the zigzag jump in the open intermediate division at the 1993 Trojan-Horse Ranch Horse Trials, Cave Creek, Arizona. Commander's rider, Shari Humble-Lamb from Las Vegas, Nevada, is a technical delegate and secretary of the United States Combined Training Association. The technical delegate is charged with inspecting the course to make sure it is safe for horse and rider.

Looking as much like a modern-day jouster as a three-day event rider, Shea Forrer travels cross-country on Arthur, who is caught here with all four feet off the ground, at the Centel Wayne-Dupage Horse Trials in 1992. Shea, an ardent motorcyclist and snowmobiler from Mequon, Wisconsin, rides more confidently with the helmet's added protection.

Left
Number 141, Margaret McIntosh and Carnival, at the 2,000-meter post on Phase C of speed-and-endurance day at the 1988 Essex Three-Day Event in Gladstone, New Jersey. The third of four speed-and-endurance phases, Phase C, like Phase A before it, is known also as roads-and-tracks. At the preliminary level a horse and rider must cover between 7,920 and 9,900 meters on roads and tracks at 220 meters per minute, which is about the equivalent of a trot.

In three-day eventing, the paths of glory lead to the ribbon presentation. After putting themselves and their mounts to the test in the 1992 Rolex Kentucky advanced horse trials, these competitors accept the rewards of their labors.

Mike Huber looks determined while Bacchus Kewe looks somewhat less spirited as they leave Henley's Hollow on the open preliminary cross-country course at the 1993 Trojan-Horse Ranch Horse Trials in Cave Creek, Arizona. Huber, who recently had been elected president of the United States Combined Training Association, is a veteran rider and trainer based in Texas.

After completing his first three-day event, Irish Coffee, a 17.2-hand bay gelding, gets a bath from his owner and rider Laura Chambers at Radnor in 1990. This Irish Thoroughbred–draft horse cross is a former show jumper, who was purchased in Athens, Greece, by Chambers's husband, Alex.

Right
The silhouettes belong to Charles Plumb and Landino, the eventual winners in the fall 1990 Fair Hill International Three-Day, advanced division, at Fair Hill, Maryland. Plumb, whose father, J. Michael, is a fixture on the United States Equestrian Team's three-day team, took a step out of his father's shadow in his first advanced three-day.

I first began photographing equestrian competition in the summer of 1985 when, as a freelancer, I was assigned by the weekly *Somerset Messenger-Gazette* to cover the Essex Horse Trials in nearby Gladstone, New Jersey. Although I didn't completely comprehend what I was seeing and photographing during the cross-country phase that Saturday in June, the action was fast and furious enough so that I became completely engrossed in making dynamic pictures. I was amazed that both the riders and their horses were brave enough (or crazy enough) to take on the harrowing jumps and obstacles set out before them.

During the stadium-jumping phase on Sunday, I was fascinated by how close a spectator could sit to the jumps—experiencing the physical and emotional bond shared by competitors and their mounts. Also impressive was the stamina and drive to win that each horse and rider demonstrated, especially after the grueling pace of the previous day.

Sally Ike and Roxboro were the eventual winners at Essex, and the following week the *Messenger* fea-

tured seven or eight shots, my first-ever published equine images.

Somerset, my home county in New Jersey, is very horse-oriented, so during the rest of that summer and fall I kept my feet wet shooting polo scrimmages and matches at the Burnt Mills Polo Club and at the major driving event held at the United States Equestrian Team headquarters, Hamilton Farm.

I like to immerse myself in in-depth photo essays about specific subjects. Thinking I was onto something new with the horses, I decided to get some direction regarding potential markets for my photos from people already involved in the horse industry. In the spring of 1986, a chance phone call led me to Susan Stilgenbauer (now Susan Benson) at Beval Saddlery in Gladstone. Bevals is the horse world equivalent of Abercrombie & Fitch, and Susan was Bevals's marketing director. An accomplished horsewoman from Brookville, Long Island, Susan knew firsthand about riding and the horse show world. She liked my ideas, added several of her own, and we formulated a plan to

Left
On a great, mountain morning in the Great Northwest, the steam also rises from Santa Cruz (foreground), being cooled out by rider Linda Dubee of Tualatin, Oregon. The pair has just completed the senior training-level cross-country phase at the 1992 Mountain Meadows Horse Trials, at North Bend, Washington.

photograph dressage, eventing and grand prix competitions at every available opportunity. As we photographed more events, our files grew and we started marketing our photos to ad agencies, design firms, equipment suppliers and magazines with considerable success. Subsequently, my photos have been used to illustrate dozens of stories in (and covers of) publications, including *The Chronicle of the Horse, Equus, Horse Illustrated, HorsePlay, Practical Horseman* and, most notably, *Spur.*

With encouragement from editors and friends, Susan and I decided to direct our efforts to creating a book of equestrian images. In the spring of 1992 we signed a contract with Howell Book House. During the next two years Susan and I traveled to Pennsylvania, Kentucky, Michigan, Illinois, Florida, California, Washington, Arizona and Alberta, Canada, to complete the shooting for this book.

Photography enthusiasts may like to know that I use Canon cameras and lenses exclusively for my 35mm work. Specific models include the F1, T90 and autofocus EOS-1, with a vast array of lenses ranging from 20mm to 300mm. My choice of film stocks for this project (with the exception of Kodak Ektapress color negative film used at the National) were exclusively Fujichrome 50, 100 and Fujichrome Velvia Professional transparency.

Alex Capozza with his pony Cupid.

If you would like to learn more about the sports of eventing, dressage or show jumping, contact the governing organizations of these disciplines for information on membership and/or spectating.

American Horse Shows Association
220 East 42nd Street
New York, NY 10017-5876
(212) 972-2472

United States Combined Training Association
461 Boston Road
Suite D6
Topsfield, MA 01983
(508) 887-9090

United States Dressage Federation
P.O. Box 80668
Lincoln, NE 68501-0668
(402) 434-8550

United States Equestrian Team
Pottersville Road
Gladstone, NJ 07934
(908) 234-1251

The United States Pony Clubs, Inc.
4071 Iron Works Pike
Lexington, KY 40511
(606) 254-7669

ACKNOWLEDGMENTS

Many people helped us in creating this book. We especially would like to thank Bill Cousins, Shari Humble-Lamb, Cathy Morelli, Peggy Murray, James Leslie Parker, Linda Kuenzler at the United States Dressage Federation, Jo Whitehouse at the United States Combined Training Association and Stephanie Macejko at the American Horse Shows Association for the information they cheerfully provided. Also, we would like to thank all the riders, trainers and owners who shared their experiences and their expertise with us.

"Now the sun is laid to sleep," pinched from the sky by two show jumping fence rails. Come sunrise tomorrow, these rails will be in place on the jumper course, and the sun will be at its usual station, smiling once again on the horse show world.